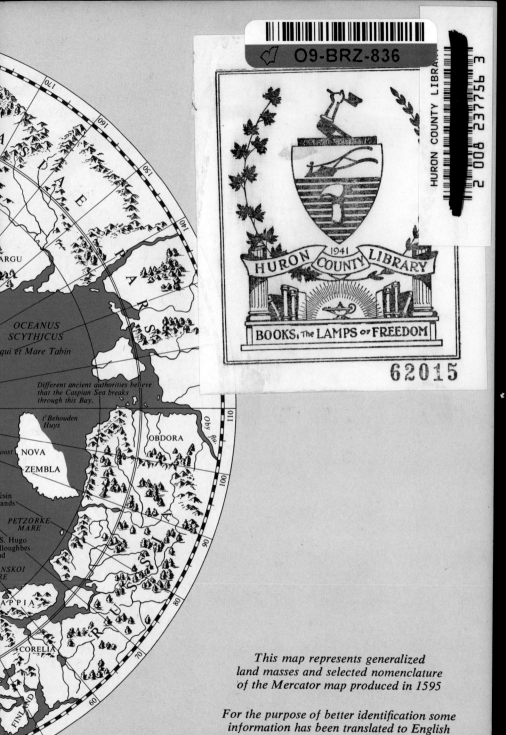

170

160

150

140

ARGU

*OCEANUS
SCYTHICUS*

qui et Mare Tabin

*Different ancient authorities believe
that the Caspian Sea breaks
through this Bay.*

*t' Behouden
Huys*

oost

NOVA
ZEMBLA

*csin
ands*

*PETZORKE-
MARE*

*S. Hugo
lloughbes
d*

*NSKOI
RE*

APPIA

CORELIA

FINLAND

50

60

70

80

90

100

110

Oby flu.

OBDORA

This map represents generalized
land masses and selected nomenclature
of the Mercator map produced in 1595

For the purpose of better identification some
information has been translated to English

ILLUSTRATIONS

2

3

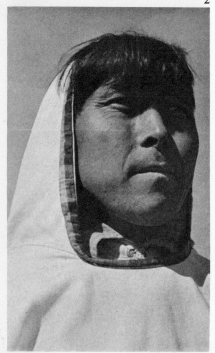

4

5

6

7

8

9

11

12

13

14

16

17

18

20

21

22

23

24

25

26

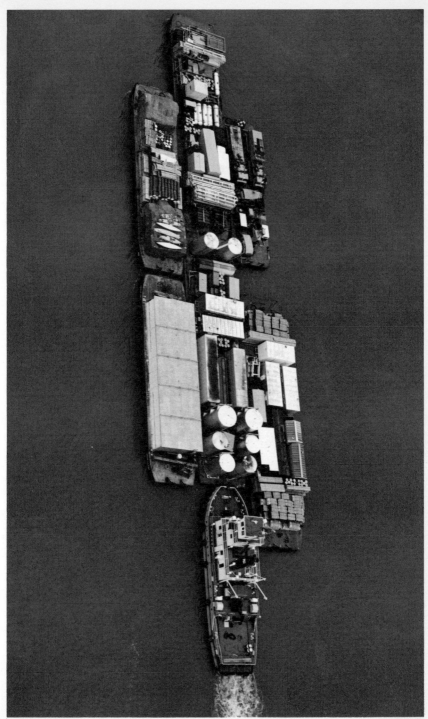

The old old Wish.

ESKIMO IN THEIR KAYAKS   PEELS RIVER
MATHERS PHOTO EDMONTON

28

People of Light and Dark

Department of
Indian Affairs and Northern Development

Issued under the authority of the
Honourable Arthur Laing, P.C., M.P., B.S.A.,
Minister of
Indian Affairs and Northern Development

People of Light and Dark

Foreword by His Royal Highness
Prince Philip

Introduction by
R. Gordon Robertson

Edited by Maja van Steensel

Dedicated to the Memory of
Superintendent Henry Asbjørn Larsen
Skipper of the St. Roch

Acknowledgements

Diane Armstrong,   Editor of *north* magazine for valuable editorial assistance.

Darrell Eagles,   Editor, Canadian Wildlife Service for assistance in the search for a colour cover.

Rev. E. Gareau, O.M.I.,   Head of the Department of Classics, University of Ottawa for translating the mediaeval Latin on the map after Mercator 1595.

Norman Hallendy,   Photographic Library, National Film Board for pictorial guidance.

T. E. Layng,   Chief, Map Division, Public Archives for obtaining copy of Mercator Map 1595.

Hélène Nantais,   Information Division, National Health and Welfare for consultation.

W. E. Taylor, Jr.,   Chief archaeologist, National Museum of Canada for assistance in contacting several contributors.

Marina Robillard,   Staff officer, Department of Indian Affairs and Northern Development for smoothing my way through the labyrinth of government.

and finally,

Dr. G. F. D. Heseltine,   without whose support and constant prodding there would not even have been the radio series.

To all these, my most sincere thanks.

MAJA VAN STEENSEL

The following essays, originally written as
radio talks, were broadcast over
the Northern Service of the Canadian Broadcasting
Corporation under the title
"The Changing North" and were produced
by Maja van Steensel in co-operation with
the National Museum of Canada.

Contents

Foreword

To most people living in the relatively comfortable temperate
areas of Canada, the north remains something of a
mystery. The most obvious features of its history, the romantic
tales of the gold rush and of trappers and explorers,
and the more prosaic accounts of its potential mineral wealth are
all more or less common knowledge. Yet the north has a
history going back 20,000 years to the first men to cross the Bering
Strait on their way south. Four thousand years ago
men first started to carve out an existence for themselves in
this unpromising area. Two hundred years ago the first Europeans
began to penetrate and make contact with the Indians and
Eskimos. These have since been followed by prospectors and
miners, government servants and scientists, priests and teachers.

This book is the second in a series and it is compiled,
like the first, from the studies and experiences of people who are
fascinated by the north as a land with its own unique
history, its particular problems and the challenge it represents
to men of courage and adventure.

My own experience of the north is rather limited but what I did
see of such places as Dawson City and Whitehorse,
Coppermine and Yellowknife, Churchill and Goose Bay and of the
vast countryside which I saw from the comfort of
an aircraft in summer was quite enough to give me a
lasting interest in this remarkable land
and in the people who live and work there.

This book is the story of and a tribute to
the people who have made the north a real part of Canada.

Buckingham Palace, 1966

People of Light and Dark

R. GORDON ROBERTSON

Introduction

At a time when so much of the world is involved in the torments of change, it is hardly surprising that the Canadian north should be changing too. It is, and changing rapidly. And yet to the observer from outside, the question that arises is whether to be surprised that the north has changed so much — or that it has changed so little.

With the exploding numbers of humanity pressing into all corners of the earth, with the development of cities, factories, roads, air-fields, apartments and all the paraphernalia that our complex way of life requires, and changing the face and the character of even remote parts of the world, the endless empty miles of the north can seem like an unique assertion of the unchanged and unchanging past, still prevailing in at least one part of the globe. It is still possible to travel for days in the north with the knowledge that no other human being is within a hundred miles. It is possible to see caribou migrate over endless miles of empty tundra; to see Eskimos travel by komatik with no motive power but their own muscles and the strength of their dogs; to watch a man stand for hours beside a seal hole, armed only with a harpoon, his patience and his skill. There are still many Indian families whose source of livelihood is the hunt and whose ways are those that have been handed down from past ages with little change. In a crowded, noisy, mechanized world the observer can only marvel that any place on earth — especially a place next-door to the wealthiest and most technically-advanced country of all time — should be so unaltered.

All that is true, and yet it is quite misleading and, in a sense, quite false. The face of the north has changed little: it is too vast to change quickly, perhaps to change ever, and man, even armed with bulldozers and power shovels, is too puny to do more than make a few scratches on the surface. But our modern methods and values are not too puny to affect profoundly the way of life and people who had, like the world in which they lived, changed little until now. We have seen in many parts of the world the revolutionary effect of the assault of our western society on the lives of people who have had no experience of it. Nowhere is that shock more profound than in our own north. We have seen too the way the appetite of our industrial society can, with the aid of modern transportation, carry the search for minerals, oil, gas, and other raw materials into the most remote and inhospitable corners of the world. The Canadian north is not the most remote of areas — although certainly it is not noted for the warmth or hospitality of the environment it affords. However, human ingenuity and technology can overcome even the rigours of the arctic. The protective shields of ice and cold, of distance and of cost no longer stand as impassable barriers to the north. And as they have ceased to hold the rest of the world at bay, the full force of our methods and machines, of our *mores* and our manners, and of our standards, whether of ethics or of material existence, has struck the north and its people.

It is not surprising that so little has changed in the past. The harshness of the north kept its native people at a subsistence level that prevented the growth of an advanced culture. They made the area unattractive for settlement and unprofitable for development. Only the fur trade provided much economic attraction and it fitted well with the established way of life. The missionaries brought changes in beliefs: a religion with a gentler view of life and new values. But these did not change much of the outer life, and one can be pardoned for a certain scepticism as to how much they changed inside. In any event, the alterations to the way of life of the north were slight until the last 20 years. Even the war left little mark: a few air bases where Eskimos had a first contact with our "outside" ways of living; more bustle and construction in the Yukon, where bustle and construction had come and gone 50 years before; some winter roads, a uranium mine and some pipelines in the Mackenzie Valley — but for most of the north, nothing.

It was after the war that the real change began, stimulated by many factors. The demand for minerals pushed prices up, and the development of more efficient methods brought costs of transportation and production down. The north became increasingly possible and interesting as a source of products other than furs and gold. The ladies' and gentlemen's styles that went with heated automobiles and the growth of urban life, along with the prohibitive labour costs involved in fur coats, together drove the prices of raw furs down. This crisis in the staple cash item of the people of the north coincided, but was otherwise unconnected with a collapse of their other staple, the caribou. For a variety of reasons, some still not fully understood, the once great numbers of the caribou, on which so much of life had depended, declined sharply. Life on the land became increasingly precarious at precisely the time that the numbers of native people began to go up — a result of better hospital and health services, welfare provisions and family allowances, and the new morality of the missionaries that excluded ancient practices of child exposure and other means by which human numbers were controlled. The crisis of the moment and of the future was apparent. The people who could not live on the land gathered more into settlements where assistance was available, something which helped in the education of their children. But they, in the process, lost both the opportunity to live the life of their fathers and their mothers and the skills to permit them to do it. For these and other reasons the "old way of life" would have proved inadequate even without the impact of the advanced economy and society from "outside."

At the same time as the old ways tottered under blows from within, the outside world became interested — again for a variety of reasons. The Canadian consciousness of national maturity and national obligation, combined with a growing sense of responsibility for the welfare of other people, led to a new interest in the people of the north — and in ways to provide education, health, housing and economic improvements. Air transportation and, in some areas, roads from the south made all parts accessible. Improved knowledge of mineral resources and of the extent of future demands pushed development into areas previously untouched. Communities developed with new problems of their own — problems for the people who came from the south and problems for the people of the north. The ordinary problems of southern living were complicated by climate, distance, sparseness of population and high costs. The problems of a native population, already beset by difficulties, were complicated by new and bewildering developments for which their culture and background afforded no preparation or guide.

The north is not unique either in the fact or in the source of change. The changes there, like the changes in Africa, Asia and other parts of the world have not come because anyone consciously decided that they should. They have come, essentially, from developments that have made the world a single community. No longer can geography and distance, or problems of transportation and communication, separate and isolate people. The world in its new contiguity is suddenly aware of the grave problems that arise when people must cope with situations for which they are unprepared and with new values and ways of thought. The tensions between the rich who grow richer and the poor who are more aware of the differences — and more aware of their claim to better treatment — have probably still to produce the full agony that must be faced before the new world community can produce the solutions that have gradually been accepted in our nation states. In microcosm, if anything as vast as the north can be called a microcosm, Canada has within its own boundaries the world problems of differing cultures, races, economies, standards and values. It has too all the problems that they bring when change is too rapid for a generation to absorb it and the old stand by, bewildered and lost, while the young try to cope, confused and apprehensive.

But this is only one side. The other side is the excitement of accelerating development in an area that until now has slept and waited. One of the last frontiers on earth holds out the hopes and provides the challenging frustrations that go with the development of a new land. Canadians first became aware of these possibilities in the 'fifties and became intrigued by them. They knew little of the north except what they had heard of exploration and the fur trade. The analogy of the opening of the west was too easily applied and too much was expected too quickly. The north is not the west: the man with a quarter section, a plow and an ox will play no part in its settlement. The resources to be developed are different, the scale of operation must be vastly greater, the problems to be overcome have elements of similarity — but also fundamental points of difference. Unless these things are understood, and unless there is a better comprehension of the north as it is now and as it is becoming, Canadians are unlikely to assess rightly either the policies to be applied or the prospects to be expected. *The Unbelievable Land* was an important contribution to a better knowledge of the north and its reception has been a measure of the need for such a volume. The present collection of studies complements the first in its analysis of the human element within the geographical setting. The authors know their north; they are up-to-date; and they understand what is going on. They are well qualified to portray to Canadian and other readers the forces of change, the hopes and the fears, the problems and the opportunities, the joys and the sorrows of an exciting but little-known land. Nothing in the north has ever been easy, and nothing is ever likely to be. If this book gives a better understanding of the dimensions and the nature of the human aspects of the northern drama it will serve an important purpose.

DR. W. E. TAYLOR, JR.

... and then came MAN

*People have lived in the arctic for over 5,000
years. They survived the harshness of the
climate, they fed and clothed themselves, no
small feat in the stark and tortured tundra.*

Squashing 5,000 years of Eskimo prehistory into these few pages
seems, to me, an untidy task, made little easier by adopting a
cavalier disregard for the fact that archaeologists as yet know little
enough of the subject. Nevertheless, the available bits of this puzzle
do suggest a continual, usually slow, culture change in the prehistoric Canadian Eskimo way of life. It must have been so for, of
course, no culture is ever static. That of the Eskimo, however
channelled by its own traditions and conservative ethos, however
restricted by its extreme environment, was a flexible culture, one
that shifted remarkably with the gross changes in seasons and adjusted to the many variations of environment across the arctic
world. Further, prehistoric Eskimo culture responded to influences
from other regions and to the gradual climatic changes of the past
50 centuries. I should stop here for a moment to explain something
of the origin of the word "Eskimo." It is an English corruption, of
a French corruption, of a Cree Indian word meaning approximately,
"eaters of raw flesh." And the Eskimo, who held the Indian in no
higher regard, called him "adlit," or louse egg, but refer to themselves with laconic pride as "inuit," the people.

To study Eskimo origins the archaeologist must define Eskimo
culture and that is not as easy as it seems. Usually, the prehistorian
considers the Eskimo pattern to entail a distinctive culture adapted
to the treeless region — to the tundra — and including a mixed hunting economy showing considerable ability in the hunting of sea

1

mammals, such as seals, bearded seals, walrus, and whale. Using such a definition, the earliest known proto-Eskimo are those of the Cape Denbigh Flint complex of northwestern Alaska. This complex dates to about 3000 B.C., at which time its people summered on the Bering Strait coast and hunted seal there, perhaps with the use of boats, while other Denbigh people lived in interior Alaska subsisting mainly on caribou. The Denbigh people are known almost solely from their flint tools, scrapers, points, bone-working tools, gouging tools, knife blades and so on. Among them are some of the most delicately chipped, precisely formed, chipped-stone tools in the entire prehistoric world. Denbigh types and styles show enough similarity to older Asian sites that most workers believe that much of Denbigh origin lies in the Palaeolithic and the Mesolithic periods of the Far East and in the early Neolithic, say about 4000 B.C., of Siberia. Some influence may also have come to Denbigh from earlier Indian cultures to the south in the North American interior. Whatever their precise origins, Denbigh people and their descendants were well-equipped to survive in the arctic. Their adaptive success is obvious in the speed with which they spread eastward across arctic Canada to northeast Greenland which they reached by 2000 B.C. By that time their vast, thin drift of population had spread down the west side of Hudson Bay to Churchill and through Baffin Island to the Ungava Peninsula.

In Canada this first period of human occupation is called Pre-Dorset, and these east-drifting Pre-Dorset descendants of the Denbigh people must have been on the central arctic coast of Canada not later than 2500 B.C. Their culture stage lasted in Canada until approximately 800 B.C., and in southwestern Greenland until about 500 B.C. Of these people we know rather more than we do about Denbigh for in the permafrost of the Canadian arctic far better preservation conditions prevail. Pre-Dorset people lived in small, widely-scattered, seasonally nomadic bands who used skin tents in summer, and small villages of partly underground huts in winter. They used toggling harpoons to hunt seal and walrus, and bows and arrows for caribou. They also, of course, speared fish and collected birds. Their extensive array of chipped flint tools clearly echoes their Denbigh ancestry, although the tools themselves are not as well formed as those of the Denbigh culture. By about 800 B.C. Pre-Dorset had evolved into what the archaeologist calls Dorset culture, a distinctive descendant of Pre-Dorset. Although the two are basically alike and similar in many details, Dorset is recognizably different in many other details important to the archaeologist, if to no one else. Characteristic items include needles, harpoon heads, lances, fish spears, soapstone lamps, and a wide range of chipped-stone tools. Unlike Pre-Dorset, Dorset sites also include ground slate points, and this is an idea that may have been borrowed by the Dorset people from prehistoric Indians living in the forest region to the south.

The oldest relics of human bone yet found in arctic Canada date to about 500 B.C., and come from a Dorset site on the south side of Hudson Strait. These scraps of bone suggest that the Dorset people were physically Eskimo. Their many sites, the thousands of artifacts collected from them, their distinctive hunting economy, and their very distinctive, small-scale, elegant art reveals their culture to be clearly in the Eskimo pattern.

Some of the "Skraelings" encountered by Leif Ericson in Vinland were surely Newfoundland Dorset Eskimo, for Dorset sites are spread widely from Coronation Gulf in the west to Newfoundland Island and eastern Greenland in the east. Dorset lasted from about 800 B.C. to about 1300 A.D. in some areas, but it began to be crowded off the arctic stage about 900 A.D. by a new culture, Thule, which was then pushing east by migration from northern Alaska eventually to reach Greenland and Labrador. Thule people and Thule culture developed from a long, evolutionary sequence of Eskimo cultures in Alaska, a sequence in part traceable back to the old Denbigh Flint complex of 3000 B.C. We do not yet know very much about the nature of the Dorset-to-Thule transition, but there was likely some cultural exchange between the two. In fact, it is quite likely that Thule people learned to make snow houses from their Dorset predecessors, for such dwellings seem a purely Canadian invention, being absent from the Alaskan variants of Eskimo culture. Although Dorset and Thule were basically rather similar in their tundra adaptation, there were major differences between them. First, Thule people had a more effective arctic adaptation, and this is best seen in their possession of the full range of gear for hunting the great baleen whales, a major food supply never available to the Dorset people who lacked the various techniques, including the umiaks, by which baleen whales were hunted. Indeed, whaling is the most distinctive feature of Thule culture, and artifacts of baleen and whale bone are very common in Thule sites. Thule people were classic Eskimo in race, in language and in culture. They used a complete range of Eskimo tools and weapons, including typical fur clothing and boots, kayaks, sleds, and sled dogs, umiaks, snow houses, soapstone lamps and pots, harpoons, bows, spears, lances, the shaman's drum, even the typical toys, such as the ajaqaq. They undoubtedly had religious, social and intellectual systems much like those of recent Canadian Eskimo life. Their first appearance on the historic stage, that is to say, within the time of written records, occurs in the accounts of Martin Frobisher, for when he was shot in the buttocks by an Eskimo arrow at Frobisher Bay, that arrow was thrown at him by a Thule culture Eskimo.

Thule people were the direct physical and cultural ancestors of the recent and the modern Canadian Eskimo including the Caribou Eskimo, who turned to the interior west of Hudson Bay. The collapse of Thule whaling explains much of the difference between Thule and recent Eskimo. It seems that in the 18th century whaling was largely abandoned in the Canadian arctic. With that decrease in their food resources, Thule people had to abandon their large, permanent, winter villages of sturdy houses made of whale bone, sods and stone slabs. They had then to take up a more nomadic life as they became increasingly dependent on the smaller, more scattered seal and walrus. This subsistence shift demanded a much wider use of the snow house and especially of the snow house village on the sea ice in winter. A phase of colder climate from 1650 to 1850 A.D., shallower seas, and the diligence of European whalers spread over several centuries may help to explain the collapse of Thule whaling. The other major change, of course, was the arrival of the European, the explorers, the traders, missions, and governments.

From the archaeology we see 5,000 years of survival in an extremely harsh environment, survival by means of a flexible, yet tradition-centred, culture that was highly responsive to environmental change and variation, but rather little affected by foreign influences. Except when the Thule culture steam-rollered Dorset, change was gradual, and basically a matter of more, and better adapted, of the same kind of thing. After the 18th century, however, arctic culture change greatly increased in rate, extent, intensity and, even, in direction. The Eskimo's heritage, so admirably suited to his traditional life, could scarcely prepare him for the overwhelming and very foreign changes of the 20th century.

DR. WILLIAM E. TAYLOR, JR., *Chief, Archaeology Division, National Museum of Canada. Born Toronto, 1927. B.A. (Toronto), A.M. (Illinois), Ph.D. (Michigan). Archaeological field work in Ontario, Quebec, Newfoundland, Arizona, Illinois and Michigan. Archaeological survey and excavation, 1950-65, on Cornwallis, Bathurst, Somerset, Banks, Victoria, Southampton, Walrus, Coats, Mansel, Nuvuk and Sugluk islands, the Ungava coast and interior and on the western arctic coast from Cape Parry to Bernard Harbour. Publications on the nature and origin of Pre-Dorset, Dorset, Thule and Sadlermiut cultures.*

DR. RICHARD GLOVER

From the Orkney Islands to the Shores of the Hudson Bay

The lure of the north, we like to think,
drew French and English both to Canada. But
in practical terms the real lure of the north
was the beaver's skin; and the life of some of
the men who traded with the
Indians for beaver is here described.

The fur trade put Canada on the map in more ways than one; and
it was the most natural of trades.

In the 16th and 17th centuries Europe wanted furs, and has continued to want them ever since. In Canada were Indians who, thanks
to the mastery of a number of skills, most of which had been
forgotten in Europe for many centuries, could enjoy life in the
bush where an untutored European would die. All around them
were animals whose pelts provided their clothing. Then from Europe
there came Frenchmen with skills which the Indian had not acquired
– in smelting iron, in weaving cloth and making gunpowder. So
came the trade in which the Indian exchanged his furs for the Frenchmen's knives, axes, needles, muskets, ammunition and blankets. That
trade was the wealth of New France. More and more Frenchmen
took to it; and some by living among Indians acquired much of the
Indian's skill in travelling in the bush and living off the land.

Then in the 1660's two young Frenchmen, Radisson and
Groseilliers, after encountering problems in Canada, turned up in
London and sold to a number of wealthy and eminent Englishmen

the idea of getting a share of the fur harvest of the north through Hudson Bay. So was born the Hudson's Bay Company whose trading posts on the shores of that remote, and usually frozen, inland sea were the first permanent English settlements on the Canadian mainland; so too Frenchmen and Englishmen began to compete for the Indians' fur.

It would be a waste of your time to repeat the story of that competition; it was part of your high school course anyway, and you know the contest between traders from Hudson Bay and traders from the St. Lawrence, continuing after the cession of Canada to Britain, lasted till the two rival companies united in 1821. So instead of repeating your school history, it seems better to write about the life you would have lived if you had been a fur trader yourself; and as this book intends to deal with the north, it will be natural to concentrate on the traders in Hudson Bay, rather than the Montrealers of the North West Company.

Very well then, consider yourself, at any date between the late 1600's and a fairly late period in the 1800's to be a young man put ashore somewhere in Hudson Bay. You will have come in a sailing ship, which started from the Thames in May. But you would be unlikely to board the ship till June when she would arrive at Stromness in the Orkney Islands, which for so many decades provided many of the men of the Hudson's Bay Company. You would join the Company partly because so many of your fellow Orkneymen were already in it; partly because it offered you a chance to save money; and — grim as this may sound — partly because life on the flat and bleak shores of Hudson Bay probably offered you a higher standard of living than you were likely to enjoy in your native Orkneys. For at the Bayside clothing, meals, fuel and shelter of a sort were provided by your employer.

The first surprise awaiting you on shore beside the Bay would almost certainly be the trees. They are by no means the finest trees that grow in Canada and there are not many species of them; but at least they are trees, of which there are few indeed among the little fields and heather-clad moors of the Orkney Islands. And the houses would provide another surprise for you, for the buildings of the trading post, built of log laid on log, were quite unlike the stone cottages of Orkney. But you would not be left to enjoy the novelty of this new land in idleness for very long. Little time would be lost in starting you on the round of hard work, which would be your chief defence against boredom in the years of your new life ashore in a new land.

First, there was the ship to be unloaded; and that had to be done fast. Though the Hudson's Bay Company ships sailed from the Thames in May, it was usually August before they came to anchor off Moose Factory, Fort Albany or York Factory; and I say "came to anchor." They were not docked, for there were no docks. Of the rivers that flow into the Bay only the Churchill has enough depth of water to be a safe harbour for ocean-going ships. So the cargo of trade goods from England had to be unloaded into small boats and then rowed or sailed ashore; and the season's fur harvest had to be ferried back to the ship. Once this job was done, the ship had to hurry home before ice made the navigation of those northern waters difficult or impossible.

When the ship was gone, the men at your trading post settled down to their winter jobs. Some, like the carpenter, the blacksmith, and the tailor who made clothes for the Indian trade, would be employed at the post. But most were employed out in the bush. The first job was lumbering, felling timber and hauling it to the river's edge. There the felled logs would lie till the spring; and when the river opened again and the ice had gone out they could be floated downstream to provide the post with its fuel for the following winter.

The next outdoor job was hunting; and there were of old, three principal hunting seasons of the Bay — the winter hunt, the spring hunt, and the autumn hunt.

The winter hunt was for rabbits and the birds which the traders called partridges and naturalists call ptarmigan. The ptarmigan is a grouse which turns white in winter and migrates south from the northern barrens to winter in flocks by the Bayside.

Every weekend the men employed out in the bush would come home to the fort; and the hunters would haul back their week's catch of partridges and rabbits.

These winter hunts were important in two ways; they provided cheap food and the food was wholesome, because it was fresh, not salted, meat. You needed fresh meat at a season when no fruit and no fresh vegetables were to be had. In the days before canning was known, meat could only be preserved by salting it; and salt meat causes the dread disease of scurvy.

On Monday morning hunters and lumbermen would go back to their daily jobs in the bush and to sleep for the next five nights in tents pitched amid the northern snow. To the winter hunting one must add fishing, with nets set under the ice.

As spring drew on, the winter flocks of ptarmigan began to thin out and move away to their still more northern breeding grounds; and after the ptarmigan had gone, the wild geese arrived. Some geese breed all around the Bay and further south too, of course. Many more breed still further north and pause only briefly in the marshes by the Bayside posts. These great migrating flocks of Canada Geese, Snow Geese and Blue Geese provided during their brief stay, first, the spring hunt; and on their return south in the fall they provided the autumn hunt. Very great numbers were shot at both seasons; and in warm spring and autumn weather all geese that could not be promptly eaten had to be salted in casks of brine. Those with experience report that salted goose is one of the less inspired of meals.

Summer was the time for kitchen gardening, to raise greens to keep men fit and free from scurvy in the season when most salt pork and salt beef from England, and salt goose too, were eaten. Summer also was the time when hay had to be made for such cattle as were kept at the posts. There were not usually many of them; but as we do not today think of Hudson Bay as a ranching country it is surprising to learn that in 1703 Fort Albany had over a hundred head of cattle.

It was in summer in the old days, before the Hudson's Bay Company men had established posts inland across the continent, that the great brigades of Indians in their birch-rind canoes came down to trade, paddling down those rivers which were the great highways of the primitive wilderness. And at last in August the annual ship from London would appear again, and your first year in the north was finished.

DR. RICHARD GLOVER, *Director of Human History Branch, National Museum of Canada. Born Cambridge, England, 1909. War service in Canadian Army. B.A., Balliol College, Oxford, 1931. Lecturer in history at the University of Saskatchewan, 1931-32; Ph.D., Harvard, 1936. Master Trinity College School, Port Hope, 1936-41. Professor of history at the University of Manitoba, 1946-63.*

DR. JAMES W. VANSTONE

Influence of European Man on the Eskimos

The Eskimos are faced with the difficulty
of accepting the 20th century
after generations of nomadic living.
To what extent has the white man influenced
their culture and way of life?

The mention of Eskimos may bring to mind a bleak, desolate expanse of snow, with a sled trail in view, and an Eskimo clinging to the back of a dogsled as he hauls home a freshly killed seal. An image of this sort would not be inaccurate even today, but it represents only a part of modern Eskimo life. The old Eskimo way of life, like the ways of most primitive peoples throughout the world today, is gone forever. This is sad; the disappearance of a unique culture is always cause for regret. At the same time, some of the harshness has been taken out of living in the arctic, and even the most conservative Eskimo would not want to return to the days before Europeans arrived in his country. The white man brought new objects and ideas to the Eskimos, and more often than not, these have been accepted enthusiastically. But these innovations have brought with them new and unprecedented problems.

Eskimos are still the most widely dispersed aboriginal peoples in the Americas. They are found from Greenland to Alaska, into the Soviet arctic, and total about 55,000 individuals. Most Eskimos, wherever they are, have been drawn into a trapping and trading economy, but they usually rely upon wild animals and fish as their main source of food. The seal is still the single most important food animal for most Eskimos, although in some regions salmon and walrus or whales may be locally significant.

Eskimos everywhere are today primarily village dwellers living in small isolated settlements, although the Canadian Eskimos were not always as sedentary as they are at the present time. Like most primitive peoples who hunted and fished for their livelihood, they moved in small bands within a fixed radius, frequenting favourite haunts, but rarely tied themselves down to definite localities. Today these wanderers have settled down in permanent villages, not one of which is of their own choosing. It was white men who chose the sites because they were readily accessible by sea, possessed safe anchorages, and were centred in areas sufficiently well populated to be profitable to the trader and the missionary. Often these settlements were so situated that the resources — the fish, seal, caribou — of the immediate environment could not provide enough food to support their populations for more than a very short time. Thus the inhabitants came to rely heavily on imported foods.

The Canadian Eskimos first encountered Europeans about the year 1000 A.D., when some Icelanders pushed westward from newly colonized Greenland and skirted the coast of Labrador. Here they met and fought with the mysterious people they called "Skrael-ings." In the 16th century, European fishermen began to pursue the cod that frequented the waters off eastern Canada, and to settle along the shores of Newfoundland and on the southern coast of the Labrador peninsula. However, except in this Atlantic coast area, the Eskimos rarely came into continuous contact with the Europeans until the 19th century. In the first half of that century, the search for a northwest passage, and later for the vanished expedition of Sir John Franklin, familiarized explorers and the world at large with the North American arctic and with the people who lived there.

Whalers followed the explorers into the arctic's eastern and western seas and many maintained shore fishing stations which employed Eskimos. At some of these stations, the Eskimos were supplied with steel traps and encouraged to devote part of their time during the winter to trapping foxes, animals that had no food value and, in pre-European times, had been virtually worthless. In this way the fur trade first came to parts of arctic Canada. It was on the southern half of Baffin Island and along the western coast of Hudson Bay that the whalers had the most pronounced effect on the Eskimo culture. Metal pots and pans, garments of cotton and wool, summer tents and canvas, fire-arms, clinker-built boats, all replaced their aboriginal Eskimo-made counterparts. As Diamond Jenness, the well known student of Eskimo culture has written, "A new generation of Eskimos arose that lacked the ancient skills and hunting lore of its parents, a generation that had lost its autarky and could hardly survive without contact with the civilized world." The decline of whaling at the beginning of the present century coincided with the rise in importance of the fur trade, and the Eskimos were drawn rapidly into a trapping-trading economy. They increasingly looked to the small arctic fur-bearers, particularly the white fox, for the income needed to obtain the guns, ammunition, cloth, and all other goods of civilization they could no longer do without.

The missionaries began to play an increasing role in the lives of the people. They learned the Eskimo language in order to perform their religious duties, and with that knowledge, they rapidly became the Eskimos' advisers, not in spiritual matters alone, but in their relations with the trader and other white men who could not understand their language. In the absence of government too, they became the educators of Eskimos, teaching the children to read and write. In the western arctic, Eskimos learned to write their language in letters of the English alphabet, while in the east a syllabic system of writing first developed by a Methodist missionary among the Cree Indians was used. The missionary and trader thus worked together to bring the world of civilization to the Canadian arctic, while the federal government in Ottawa remained largely unconcerned.

During the first three decades of the 20th century, widely-separated police posts were established in the arctic, and the Royal Canadian Mounted Policeman became a familiar figure during inspection trips to Eskimo villages. The Canadian government was slow to accept the responsibility for its Eskimo citizens and to extend to them the benefits enjoyed by other Canadians in the urban areas to the south. Since about 1950, however, much progress has been made and much money spent in an effort to solve the many problems faced by a people who no longer can return to their old ways of life, and who are as yet only partially adjusted to the new.

Schools and hospitals have been built, and other services provided. Many health problems have been solved, and it has been generally recognized that education and training for wage employment are the two basic needs which must be met if the Eskimos are to lead useful lives in their own environment in a modern world. In some parts of the arctic the Eskimos have seen 2,000 years of technology compressed into two decades, as radar domes arose by the side of igloos. But the history of the contact between Eskimos and whites shows that the Eskimos have been willing to accept the artifacts and ideas if they will help him adjust to his changing physical, economic and social environment. An understanding of how the ideas and objects brought by the white men have influenced his way of life can assist both "Innuit" and "Kabloona" to bridge the painful gap between the old and the new ways of life.

DR. JAMES W. VANSTONE, *Associate Curator of North American Archaeology and Ethnology, Chicago Natural History Museum. Born Chicago, 1925. B.A., Oberlin College, 1948; M.A., University of Pennsylvania, 1950; Ph.D., University of Pennsylvania, 1954. Taught in Dept. of Anthropology, University of Alaska, 1951-59; University of Toronto, 1959-66. Field work in Alaska and Northwest Territories with Eskimos and Chipewyan Indians.*

DR. C. D. ELLIS

Influence of the Missionary

*No account of the evolution of
Indian and Eskimo people can fail to take
into consideration the effects of
the missionary on traditional values.*

Ordinarily, one thinks of a missionary as someone primarily concerned with the communication of religion. Religion is part of the overall way of life, or as we say of the culture of a people, and a very important part of that way of life too. Religion has a bearing not merely on the god people pray to, but on the persons they can marry, the food they can eat, the work they can do and even when they can do it. Whether the religion happens to be Christianity or something else, it usually expresses the meaning people see in life, and in the process of doing this, it gives some kind of expression to the standards people live by. Naturally enough then, people tend to understand their religion in terms of life as they know it. We still sometimes say "The Lord is my shepherd", in the language of a sheep-herding community, when in fact to some of us, in the north country at any rate, the idea might be much better expressed by "The Lord is my navigator", or "The Lord is my guide".

Religion fits into an overall perspective in the picture of life. Even though the missionary's primary concern is in the area of religious activity, we would normally expect him to speak of his faith in the terms of his own total life experience, and this would often communicate to his audience certain ideas from other parts of the missionary's background. Indeed, we would expect a change in religion on the part of any community to involve adjustments in other areas of life as well. We would look for the so-called "acculturative effects".

This, in the main, is what this chapter is all about: the cultural modifications produced, in part at least, by adjustment in the face of missionary activity. My own observations are made largely on the basis of several years residence in the eastern Canadian sub-arctic, especially in the area of James Bay. Here one may observe how the results of adjustment, both direct and indirect, to mission-ary activity, have produced their effect on nearly every level of social experience from the value system to food ways, from music and choosing a marriage partner to the technology characteristic of the culture. Let me touch on several points where the effect of the missionary may be discerned, as his culture makes its impact on the group with whom he communicates.

We might look at marriage patterns first. Among the Cree people and other northern Algonquian groups there appears to have been at one time an established pattern of marrying cross-cousins: that is, father's-sister's child, mother's-brother's child. References to this occur in the literature, many old-timers in the north and the west are familiar with the practice, and in some bands, the name for male cross-cousin and brother-in-law, or alternatively, female cross-cousin and sister-in-law are identical. Today the custom is in various stages of break-down due to a variety of factors; but more con-servative members of many communities still seem to feel that some kind of cousin linkage is appropriate in the selection of a marriage partner.

At one settlement, I recall a curious situation which developed. Several young men seemed to have difficulty in locating a suitable wife, while at the next village, young, marriageable women were in better supply. Since communication between the villages was good, the missionary made the obvious suggestion. It was only later that certain considerations, which had escaped the missionary, came to light. Members of the first village tended to be conservative in attitude, and apparently still regarded some type of kinship tie (at the same generation level, naturally) as desirable for prospective marriage partners. Young adults at the neighbouring village often did not fit into this class. In the home village, on the other hand, those who did fit the kinship requirements often belonged to families which had many years before identified themselves with a different mission. Feelings in this matter ran deep among the villagers them-selves, hence a reluctance to form otherwise acceptable alliances at home. In any case, the resultant atmosphere favoured the development of alternatives to the traditional patterns in selecting a marriage partner. Substitute solutions were evolved, and some were very good. My point, however, is not to evaluate the change for good or bad, but simply to note a cultural modification stemming partly and indirectly from the missionary enterprise.

Unexpected as it might seem at first, missionary activity has in certain areas affected residence patterns as well. The desire to serve the whole man has led nearly every mission group to establish schools associated with centres of worship. These residential and bush-schools dot the northland. More than one day-school teacher, however, has complained of the difficulty of teaching students who are withdrawn from the classroom each time the family goes to the trapline. Various devices have been used to reduce these extended absences. One result has been to encourage a village pattern of residence the year round, as contrasted with periodic withdrawal to camp life. When the men-folk are away on the trapline, this often makes for altered patterns of dependency, with the missionary or trader as the point-of-call when help is required.

Again, what begins as an adjunct to missionary activity, namely the school program, ends by promoting a hierarchically organized community life, with one or a few people at the top, and the bulk in a position of semi-dependency — this, in contrast to the loosely-knit bundle of small groups more or less independent, which makes up the usual Cree band.

On reflection, it would probably appear obvious that a whole set of religious concepts, such as those of Christianity, could hardly be introduced into another society without affecting its value-system from the bottom up. The Christian evaluation of human life is one item which has gained a firm hold in the scale of what is valued and what is not.

While the evidence is slim, there are clues which point to the practice, in pre-contact times, of exposing children who were unwanted or considered too weak to survive the hardships of life. The practice could not, of course, be condoned by the Christian community. Christian teaching plus medical services, long available almost exclusively through missionary channels, have reduced the practice to near disappearance.

At this point, it is of some interest to consider pre-marital sexual behaviour on the part of members of the community we're thinking about. While deeply rooted attitudes and behaviour patterns often display a high degree of resistance to change, there may nonetheless be a growing sense that one's actual and professed standards are out of line. One area where this is the case is that of pre- and sometimes post-marital sexual behaviour. Probably the pre-European contact patterns of relatively casual sexual relations before marriage have in some areas not changed appreciably. Theoretically, members of the Christian community are aware of the ideal which, like other ideals, they realize only imperfectly. Interestingly enough, however, local custom in this respect was reinforced by accepted usage on the part of many of the servants of the Hudson's Bay Company, whose social roots were in the Highlands or Western Isles of Scotland. Here the custom of a certain controlled latitude we might call it, for the eldest unmarried daughter in the family prevailed. Similarly, in Cree circles, a certain importance has traditionally been attached to a girl's proof of fertility, and the custom has been that any offspring which may result are ordinarily absorbed into the family of the girl's mother, unless girl and sexual partner should marry first. Where post-marital disharmony arises from such an event, it is often due to the husband's having recognized the child as his own, and having subsequent doubts cast on his paternity.

Among many Indian groups, divorce is almost non-existent, but much more significant is the fact that desertion also is quite rare. On the other hand, cases of infidelity are probably higher than is shown on any available records, if village gossip and overall rates of illegitimacy are taken into account. My point is that whether the attitude be one of resistance to or promotion of the Christian standard, serious acculturation at the level of attitude has gone on to a degree and in an area calling for value judgments of a critical nature.

In the area of social controls, one traditional medium of requital, that of conjuring, has disappeared in many centres. The same cannot be said of gossip, although outright violence seems to occur only under the stimulus of alcohol. In this connection the report of one, now elderly, informant is of interest. Recalling the Hannah Bay Massacre of 1832, she remarked: "There used to be lots of murder in the bush before the missionaries came. You don't hear about that kind of thing now." Without wishing to exaggerate unduly the influence of missionary contact in this connection, it may be stated that a general awareness of Christian behavioural requirements is common, and at least outward conformity is aimed at, while many in fact observe the prescriptions of Christian living, often in conscientious detail.

Instances are on record of a missionary quite frankly aiming at making over his converts' whole way of life. The celebrated account of Duncan and the Metlakatla incident is a case in point. Taking up residence at a distance from the village at which operations were directed, the missionary encouraged converts to leave the village and settle in a new one about his own residence. Where this succeeded, new technology was often introduced, skills of reading and writing developed and the consequent level of acculturation was very high indeed.

It is perhaps in the field of education and communication that the greatest systematic effort has been made in the acculturation of Indian groups through the modification of attitudes. Not only have the three R's commonly been taught in mission schools, but the objectives which have been held before the child have been those highly regarded in the dominant, European-Canadian society. He is trained and rewarded for achieving goals often unrelated to life on the trapline, and frequently he is imbued with doubt as to the traditional values of his home milieu. As opportunities to utilize such training materialize away from home, the process of deculturation and adjustment to a new way of life is accelerated. Even the incidental confrontation with new foodstuffs on the residential school table, or from the mission garden, contributes to developing an enlarged dietary vista. When corresponding foodstuffs appear on the trader's shelves in the home village, the clientele has already been prepared.

Of all people, the missionary is one most immediately concerned with communication. The need for written materials in the language of the people is one of the first to which he must address himself. No account of the Christian translation enterprise in the Canadian north and west should omit mention of the syllabic system developed by the Reverend James Evans for transcribing Cree, and later applied to Ojibwa and Eskimo. For over a century the techniques of reading and writing have been practised by persons using this system, both for official publication and personal correspondence, a missionary-based introduction, if you will, of the habits of European culture to the Indian set of folkways. It should be noted that only a few of the many areas of acculturation have been touched on here. No judgments have been made as to the value of any culture traits adopted. That is not the purpose of this chapter. Change is part of living: the important thing is to recognize how it takes place, and under what conditions, and then to utilize this knowledge to improve the human situation to the best of one's ability.

The chapter was based on a longer paper, "The Missionary and the Indian in Central and Eastern Canada", which appeared in *Arctic Anthropology* Vol. 2, No. 2 (1964).

DR. C. DOUGLAS ELLIS, *Vice Dean and Associate Professor for the Humanities Division, Arts and Science, McGill University. Born Shawville, Quebec, 1923. B.A., McGill, 1944; M.A., University of Toronto, 1946. Granted M.A. from Yale, 1949, and B.A., Cambridge, 1951; Ph.D., McGill, 1954. Post-graduate work in linguistics at Cornell and Michigan. Field work on Cree language. Research west coast of James Bay. Taught linguistics, Dept. of Anthropology, University of Toronto. Anglican priest, Diocese of Montreal.*

PETER NICHOLS

Since the Days of Barter

*The whalers of the 19th century whetted
the Eskimo's appetite for white man's
goods. Now modern stores have replaced the
informal visits to the whaling ships.*

For the past 30 years I have spent most of my time in the Canadian
arctic and my experience in trading with native people has necessarily been limited to the Eskimos. Much the same methods were
used in dealing with the Indians — the one difference being that the
radical trading developments and changes which have taken place
in the arctic during the past 15 years occurred at a much earlier
date in Indian country.

First let us take a look at what the arctic was like in the early
days, and then to illustrate some of these changes in the trading
system I will compare life in the old days with life as it is today.

The earliest trading with Eskimos was carried on by Scottish and
American whalers who used their vessels as a base of operations
for the few months they were in the north. Trading, of course, was
incidental to the main business of whaling, but it was the start of
the whole cycle, creating among the Eskimo people the desire to
obtain the white man's goods.

The first land-operated establishments in the high arctic, occupied by traders all year round, came into being in the early part
of this century. And they were a far cry, indeed, from the modern
Hudson's Bay Company department stores in the arctic today.

To establish a trading post, company officials first located an area
known to have a fairly large Eskimo population. Then a supply
ship was sent with building materials and trade goods. A safe,
sheltered harbour in the general vicinity was found and the traders,

usually two of them, were put ashore, bag and baggage, and left to carry on as best they could. The buildings they erected were pretty primitive, wood-frame, not insulated and often poorly put together. A trading post generally consisted of three or four buildings, a dwelling for the staff (the only heated building), a store, and one or two warehouses. The store was lined with shelving on all available wall space, with counters to separate the customers from the merchandise. And the goods offered in trade consisted of the minimum basic requirements: flour, sugar, tea, tobacco, matches. Sometimes, instead of sugar, molasses was used. Stored in hundred-gallon puncheons, it was served out in the sealskin bags brought in for this purpose by the Eskimo customers.

The important section in the store was the hardware department, whose items made the Eskimo hunter's task much easier, and much less precarious. Rifles, traps, ammunition, knives, pots and pans were always in great demand, whereas food and clothing at that time still came from the bounties of the sea and land.

When the customers came to trade, they brought with them white fox pelts. It was white fox that had first lured the traders into the Barren lands. Even today this fur remains one of the two main commercial commodities exported from the arctic, the other being sealskin, which only in recent years has become an important item of trade.

In the old days the Eskimo lived in small, related family groups, scattered over hundreds of miles of coastline, and their visits to the trading post occurred only once or twice a year, great occasions, indeed, for the lonely trader as well as for the Eskimo. During the winter, the head of the family travelled alone to the post to trade. He came by dog team and spent as short a time as possible, so he could get back without delay to his dependents. During the summer, on the other hand, when the weather was fair the whole family would arrive by boat and would wait for the annual supply ship to arrive and depart before returning to their settlement.

A shopping list — the supermarket standby of the busy modern housewife — is no innovation. I can remember, 30 years ago, the Eskimos used one, carefully prepared in syllabic writing months ahead of a trading visit, and probably gone over again and again before they arrived at the post. The actual trading began with the evaluation of furs and the agreement on a price. Then trading tokens to the value of the Eskimo's furs were placed on the counter and, as the purchases were made, the tokens were withdrawn to show the customer the cost of each item. This enabled him at all times to know the amount in trade he had coming to him.

There has been a good deal of misunderstanding about the use of tokens in the fur trade. In fact, it is generally believed that they were a form of currency. This was definitely not so. The token had no monetary value. It was an easy method for the customer to keep check on his purchases. The Hudson's Bay Company used brass and, later, aluminium tokens, with the value marked on them, usually in multiples of 20 cents. Other traders preferred buttons, or thimbles, or wooden sticks of varying lengths. The Eskimo customer became very knowledgeable in the use of tokens. Great care and thought were given to their allocation on trade goods that would have to last many months before another visit to the post could be arranged.

Trading in good times, when foxes were plentiful, was a joyful occasion. Unfortunately, the white fox, being subject to cyclic fluctuations, reaches a peak of abundance every four years, then drops off to extreme scarcity. When the market value of the fox declined, and also the cycle, the trader and the Eskimo both suffered hard times. However, the responsible trader, realizing that the Eskimo's well-being was tied very closely to his own, would give credit from the store to carry over the customers until better conditions prevailed. Substantial debts were often on the traders' books for three or four years. Then, most credit advances could be collected as the white fox cycle again reached a high point and the pelts were available in quantity.

Supplies were delivered once a year by ship, and radio communication had not yet been introduced. This meant complete isolation from the outside world for the young trader. But his work in the store was only a relatively small part of his job. He was the doctor, the dentist, the advisor and welfare officer for the Eskimo. In most cases he was the only white man in the community and was expected to take action and judge wisely in any and all emergencies. The Eskimos, on the other hand, felt responsible for the white man's well-being in their land which, without question, they knew best. It is no wonder that they were justly proud of their ability to survive under the most adverse conditions. Every young man who aspired to become a trader served at least five years' apprenticeship under several experienced traders. He learned the Eskimo language and used it exclusively in his dealings with the local customers. He was promoted to trader only after he had proven himself capable of assuming responsibility in all its many phases.

What of today? Well, to begin with, one never speaks of a trader now. He is a "store manager". The old historic name of the Fur Trade Department itself has been changed: it is now the Northern Stores Department. The old methods of trading have disappeared. All store transactions are carried on in cash, the trading tokens being forgotten relics of the past. Each modern, heated store in the arctic offers self-serve groceterias, there is a cash register at the check-out counter, fluorescent lighting is used throughout the unit, and merchandise ranges from frozen TV dinners, transistor radios and fruit-flavoured lipstick to the more traditional items: coal-oil, lamps and rifles.

Eskimo tastes are changing along with every other aspect of their lives. In foods they have acquired a preference for practically all canned products . . . meats, vegetables and fruits. They are now fashion-conscious in their clothing purchases and they desire the most modern furnishings and appliances when they move into permanent homes. Schools introduced by the government began the change in the hunting and trapping economy of the people. Young men were no longer taught by their fathers to carry on their traditional pursuits. Wage-earning employment became a necessity and while sufficient jobs are still not available to take up the full labour force, many Eskimos are now employed by government agencies.

The Hudson's Bay Company has also expanded its recruitment of Eskimos for store managers and clerks. At present 53 per cent of the arctic staff of the Hudson's Bay Company is Eskimo and the rate is increasing year by year.

Isolation is no longer a factor in the far north. Practically every community is served throughout the year by at least one monthly service carrying passengers, freight and mail. In many cases there are weekly air services scheduled. The delivery of store supplies is continuous through the year by air cargo, rather than the annual shipment of goods by water. Other changes? Well, the Eskimo snow house and skin tent are now rarely seen; they've been replaced by permanent wooden houses, neatly set out in rows in each village.

The motorized toboggan or ski-doo has taken over from the dog team just as the Peterhead and the motorboat have supplanted the kayak. Co-operative stores have been introduced into the north, with Eskimos operating them under the guidance of government officials. Mail-order houses are using the improved postal facilities to the maximum and their catalogues are taking on the same importance for arctic families as for the residents in rural parts of southern Canada.

As you can see, the role of the trader has changed, like everything else in this territory. Now the modern store manager has less freedom and more routine, as he pursues his career in merchandising. He lives comfortably in a modern, centrally-heated home, equipped with hot and cold running water, attractive furnishings and electrical appliances. It is true there is less adventure nowadays, but the young storekeeper of the north can still be justly proud that he, like his predecessors, still provides a vital service to the people of Canada's final frontier.

PETER NICHOLS, *Manager, Arctic Division Hudson's Bay Company from 1933. Served at posts in Northern Quebec and Northwest Territories until moving to Head Office in 1947. Works closely with the Eskimos, speaks their language and is at home with them on their hunting trips. Still travels five months of the year in the arctic and gives frequent lectures on the north.*

DAVID GIMMER

Milady's Fur . . . the Trapper

The fur that fetches a good price at
international auctions did not get there solely
because of its fur value. If trapping
families could afford to buy pork and beef,
the display of fur might be considerably
less, and the prices could well be higher.

Someone asked me recently if the glamour and adventure had disappeared from trapping. My reply was that the glamour and
adventure, if present at all, had certainly faded but more important
is the fact that the financial rewards have all but disappeared. We
must face it, the harvesting of wild fur is not a particularly reward-
ing occupation in its present condition. Trapping in the north is
conducted primarily by Indians, Metis and Eskimos with only a
few white men still participating. Fur dealers are, however, invari-
ably white men, with only a few native people engaged in such
ancillary occupations as clerks, storesmen, and similar jobs. Numerous changes in the economic and social life of the trappers, and
within the fur industry itself, have had a profound effect on trapping
as an occupation.

In the early post-war years, fur prices boomed and where fur
stocks were available, trappers could make a fairly adequate living.
Various factors, such as increased fur production, declining demand
and competition from foreign furs and synthetics have caused a
drop in fur prices. The result has been a fairly stable market over
the past few years, but at depressed prices with only minor seasonal
variations. In the last five years considerable improvement has been
noted in long haired fur such as fox, lynx and marten, but this has
not had a marked effect on the trappers' incomes, because these

furs for the most part do not represent the bulk of their production. Beaver and mink production are considered the backbone of the wild fur industry for trappers generally, with white fox and marten displacing them in some arctic areas. In other areas, muskrat are the most important species. During this period of stable fur prices, the cost of goods and services has continued to spiral, contributing to a decline in the trappers' purchasing power. Fur prices not having kept pace with the cost of living have, in effect, declined.

One must understand the Indian and Eskimo traditional approach to trapping to realize how economic and social change has affected their lives and their occupations. To most native people, hunting was "a way of life", and they still treat it in much this way. It was customary for the entire family to move to the hunting grounds each autumn and every member of the family was familiar with his or her duties and responsibilities. In many cases fur was mainly a by-product of their hunting activities. The emphasis was placed on obtaining food from the land, and trapping for fur was not primarily an economic endeavour.

Each summer various groups would gather in the different settlements to socialize and trade, with dispersal during the winter following a fairly regular pattern. The establishment of schools, churches, stores and settlement housing has disrupted this once familiar pattern. Academic education, regular church attendance, social activities and the comforts of settlement life are not compatible with the traditional pattern of hunting and trapping. One of the things which has also affected trapping is education. The young people who attend school from the time they are five or six until possibly 16 do not receive adequate training for trapline living. When they leave school they have no real desire or experience which would fit them for a life on the trapline.

Many Indian men now travel to their traplines without their families but are reluctant to remain there for a complete season, away from the social and family life that they know when in the settlement. Others are reluctant to travel the long distances required to reach good trapping areas without their families with the result that many more distant areas now go unharvested while country close to the settlement is being over-trapped and over-hunted for big game. Trappers are making ever-increasing use of aircraft to travel to and from their traplines. This for the most part is a luxury they cannot afford, due primarily to the declining returns from fur. For example, a large group of trappers in the Northwest Territories received total returns for the 1963-64 trapping season of just over $500 each. When you consider a charter trip by aircraft costs $300 - $350, you will realize that very little is left for the trappers to meet family requirements. These are average figures; some trappers did much better financially.

I have perhaps portrayed a rather bleak picture of trapping in the north, but there are possible solutions to some of the problems outlined. It will be necessary to know more about the fur resources of the country so that trapping plans can be developed for potential fur producing areas. Cycles or fluctuations in the populations of fur bearers, such as arctic fox, marten and mink might be plotted to determine when trapping will be economically feasible. In those years when the cycles are at a low it would not be economically feasible to assist a trapper to go into an area where we are fairly certain that he would not obtain an adequate income; on the other hand, when the populations are at a high, the fur resources should be harvested. Training programs for trappers could be developed to teach trapline and fur management, pelt preparation, fur marketing and trapline economics and to encourage their full participation and involvement in a properly designed fur harvesting program.

Trapper assistance programs could be expanded to provide credit for such things as grubstakes, adequate equipment, trapline base camps and, where feasible, air transportation. A system of fur marketing might be considered which would ensure that trappers receive full market value for their fur in keeping with its quality and handling. This might include advances on fur shipped to fur auction companies and the establishment of collection depots throughout the north. To ensure the success of such a program, adequately trained staff would be required at strategic locations throughout the north to supervise the program and provide the technical competence related to fur resources management that is required. Present game officers might benefit from training in modern game management to improve their skills and enhance their contribution to the fur program.

One could write a whole book on a subject as complex as trapping in the northern areas of Canada; I have tried to outline some of the problems and suggest possible solutions to at least some of them. Perhaps this message will encourage discussion and action towards the search for a solution. I would like to state, in closing, that whatever transpires the full co-operation of everyone concerned, including trappers, traders, game administrators and other government officials will be necessary to develop an adequate fur harvesting program.

DAVID GIMMER, *Supervisor of Wildlife, Indian Affairs Branch, Dept. of Indian Affairs and Northern Development. Born Harrisburg, Ont., 1921. War service in Canadian Army and Air Force. Lumber and logging operations Northern Ontario, 1945-52. Joined Ontario Dept. of Lands and Forests. Graduate of Ontario Forest Rangers School, 1955. Wildlife conservation in Northern Ontario, 1952-58. Indian Affairs Branch, 1958.*

DR. DON CHARLES FOOTE

... of Whales and Whalers

*It is not known when men first began to hunt
whales in arctic waters north of Bering
Strait. Perhaps some whaling was carried
on nearly 3000 years ago. Certainly
native people in many places from Bering
Strait to the Mackenzie Delta hunted whales
during the last 1000 years.*

Each summer several species of whales migrate north to the western
arctic; there are the small white whales usually called beluga, a
Russian name, the Pacific killer whale, and the grey whales. Just
north of Bering Strait itself can be found the finback, the hump-
back, and probably the Pacific right whale. But the most important
large whale to frequent the region is the Greenland whale, commonly called "the bowhead."

The early whale hunters who lived north of Bering Strait were
interested primarily in the capture of white whales and bowheads.
Each spring, in late March or early April, these two species of
whale began to move north from their winter feeding grounds in the
Bering Sea and further south. Their principal migration route appears to follow the eastern coast of Siberia, through Bering Strait,
and then the western and northern coast of Alaska, eastward to the
Beaufort Sea. Normally the white whales and bowheads travel
together in early spring. By the first weeks of June, the main body
of bowheads will have passed the western Alaskan coast. White
whales continue to move northward until late June or early July.
In autumn the whales migrate westward from the Beaufort Sea past
Point Barrow and then south to Bering Strait, by way of Wrangel

Island and the waters north of the Chukchee Peninsula. The early Eskimo whalers took advantage of this migration pattern.

Until less than 100 years ago, white whales were normally caught with strong nets or harpoons. At Point Hope, Alaska, for example, long nets made from bearded seal line were strung out from the beach to catch belugas swimming near shore. Once tangled in the net, the whales were attacked with harpoons and spears from umiaks and kayaks.

The white whale was a valuable animal to people living along the sea coast and inland. Properly dried and cut, the skin could be used as boot soles, boat covers or rawhide. Dried and cooked, the skin was an excellent food. The oil was used for food, as a fuel to light the oil lamps, and as a preservative for storing meat and sometimes berries and plants. White whale meat was an excellent food, either freshly cooked or air-dried and stored in oil. Sinew from the whale made a strong thread which could be braided into strands for sewing or for the making of nets. The bones provided a raw material for a number of tools such as picks.

When we speak of the traditional Eskimo whale hunters, however, we usually mean those people who captured the large bowhead whales. In contrast to the white whale, which may grow to the length of 11 to 14 feet, and a ton or so in weight, the bowhead can be 50 to 60 feet long and weigh 60 tons. Most of the whales killed by the early Eskimos were about 30 feet long, weighing about 30 tons. Unlike the white whale, which has teeth and feeds on fairly large animals such as fish, the bowhead's mouth is equipped with several hundred long thin baleen plates which catch small marine organisms called plankton. Thus we have the strange fact that the largest animal in the north, the bowhead, lives on some of the smallest animals in the north. And the bowhead prefers to spend its time near or in the many holes and cracks of the sea ice. Rarely are these whales seen too far away from the ice.

In order to hunt the bowhead, the Eskimo sought out coastal locations close to the whales' migration route. These were often long spits or points jutting seaward from the mainland. Each spring, the men pulled their skin boats across the land-fast ice to the edge of the open sea, the shore lead. Here they waited, sometimes for days or weeks, before a bowhead surfaced near the boat. Then, in complete silence, they swiftly launched their umiaks, paddled toward the whale and at the last moment, often when the boat was touching the whale's back, the harpooner drove his weapon into the animal. Attached to the harpoon was a long line carrying three or more inflated sealskin floats. These floats helped to slow the whale's movements and to mark his location for other crews. The animal was finally killed with long-handled, stone-tipped lances. Once a bowhead was captured, it was towed to thick ice and pulled out with sealskin ropes. The black skin was eaten as a special food called "muktuk", the blubber was a source of oil for heating, light and food, the meat was eaten frozen or cooked, and the bones were utilized for numerous things, from house supports to sled runners and harpoon heads. Baleen could be shaped into fish nets, lines and ribs for a skin-boat frame. Other parts of the whale also had special purposes; for example, the thin outer layer of the liver made an excellent cover for the Eskimo drum.

It was not until the early 18th century that Europeans first began to learn of large numbers of whales around Bering Strait. But commercial whaling by Europeans and Americans did not begin until the following century. The early American whalers, usually sailing from the New England ports of New Bedford, New London, Providence and Edgartown, were joined by a few French and British ships. The Russians never developed a successful arctic whaling business. Within a few years of its start, however, whale hunting north of Bering Strait was left completely in American hands. The whalers sought out the bowheads because it was a slow-swimming animal that could be overtaken by small boats lowered from the main ship. It was also a relatively docile animal compared to the Pacific right whale or the sperm whale. Finally, it yielded more baleen and whale oil for its size than did other species of whales hunted in the north Pacific.

There is little doubt that by the mid-1860's, the bowhead whales were so scarce that whalemen began to kill walrus for oil and ivory. In just over one decade, they probably killed more than a quarter of a million of these animals. Commercial whaling in general declined after 1860. A severe blow was dealt to the industry in 1865 when, during the last days of the Civil War, the Confederate privateer *Shenandoah* captured or burned 34 ships of the arctic whaling fleet near Bering Strait. After the Civil War, coal-oil, and eventually, petroleum products were used more and more instead of whale oil.

31

But the arctic whaling industry did not die completely because the price of baleen, used in women's corsets and buggy whips, continued to increase.

In 1880, the first large steam-driven whaler joined the arctic fleet. Within a few years, a small but effective force of other steamers sailed north from San Francisco to beyond Bering Strait each year. It was in 1885 that several Americans decided to establish shore stations near the villages of Alaskan Eskimo whale hunters. The first stations were built at Point Barrow and Point Hope, followed, in the next few years, by stations at Wainwright and Point Lay. Here the Americans hired Eskimo crews and hunted the bowheads in early spring from the edge of the land ice. This whaling became known as "floe-whaling" or "floor-whaling" and continued until the first decade of the 20th century. Some floe-whaling was carried on near the Mackenzie Delta.

It was in the late 19th century that the whaling fleet slowly extended its hunting range farther eastward from Point Barrow. Finally in 1888, the first whaling ships reached Herschel Island in the Beaufort Sea. The following year the whalers over-wintered their vessels in the western Canadian arctic for the first time. This pattern of shore-based whaling in northern Alaska and over-wintering ships in the western Canadian arctic lasted until 1907 when the price of baleen fell so low that few commercial whalers remained in business. The hunting of bowheads off the Mackenzie River all but stopped at this time, although the Eskimo hunt for white whales continued. In Alaska, some few shore-based whalers and the Eskimos at Point Barrow, Wainwright, and Point Hope carried on their traditional spring hunt for the bowhead. White whales were killed at these places and at Point Lay, Kivalina, Kotzebue Sound and some points further south. American commercial whaling in the eastern arctic, around Hudson Bay, also stopped in the early 20th century.

Today the Eskimos from at least one village on the Chukchee Peninsula coast still hunt bowhead whales. In Alaska the animals are killed at Point Hope, Wainwright and Point Barrow. There is no systematic bowhead whale hunting in Canada. The Alaskan Eskimos have retained many of their former hunting methods. Every spring the men haul their skin-covered umiaks to the ice-edge with dog teams or skimobiles. When the whale is near enough to be attacked, they paddle out and strike the animal with a hand-thrown bomb-gun (or darting gun) and harpoon. Once killed, the whale is pulled on to the ice with heavy ropes and block and tackle.

The average annual kill of bowheads in arctic Alaska is probably from 10 to 15 animals. Very rarely is a bowhead killed in Canadian waters. White whales are hunted in Alaska and Canada, but now the high-powered rifle, metal-tipped harpoon and gasoline boat engine or outboard motor have replaced the traditional nets, spears and kayaks. Although half a century has passed since the bowhead was chased by the large commercial whaling ships and land-based whalers, the animal population has not yet returned to its former size. Only continued programs of careful conservation and wise use will allow this magnificent and important member of the arctic animal community to regain its rightful place among the ice floes and clear cold water of the north.

DR. DON CHARLES FOOTE, *Assistant Professor, McGill University. Born New York, 1931. B.A., Dartmouth College, New Hampshire, 1953; Master's degree in geography, 1958; Ph.D., McGill University, 1965. Research student, University of Oslo, Norway, 1953-54 and 1956-57. Senior scientist in charge of program of human geographical studies with United States Atomic Energy Commission, Point Hope, Alaska, 1959-62. Travelled extensively in northern Canada, Norway, Sweden and Finland. Presently undertaking research in northern arctic Alaska and Baffin Island.*

WILLIAM M. GILCHRIST

About our Untold Resources

*Since the turn of the century man has
searched the north for precious or
semi-precious metals, but mass movements
such as the Klondike gold rush are a
thing of the past since men have increasingly
been replaced by machines.*

In 1896 gold was discovered on a tributary of the Klondike River,
and a horde of men, and a few women, headed north. Most of them
knew only three things about the Klondike — that it was cold, that
it was remote, and that gold nuggets could be picked up from the
ground. They were right on all counts, but by the time most of them
got to Dawson, the placer ground had been staked by knowledgeable sourdoughs who had been in the country before 1896. Most of
the newcomers, city men from the United States and Canada,
drifted back south. A few stayed on; some struck it rich, but their
number was small. Others stayed to work for wages and these men
saw the steady change in the mining industry as the rich ground was
worked out. At first, a fortune in gold could be washed from the
gravel in a pan but later, shafts had to be sunk to reach pay dirt.
Gradually, the mining operations became mechanized, and large
dredges, thawing plants, railways, aqueducts, dams, pipes and
flumes were built to free the gold from the frozen ground. The
development of the Klondike gold-fields illustrates, in microcosm,
the development pattern of all northern mining: the "rush" for a
precious mineral that could be easily mined, or the staking and
exploitation of a rich localized deposit.

The basic engineering principles involved in arctic mining do not
differ from those used in more temperate climates, but arctic condi-

tions have an impact on the application of these principles. Distance, terrain and climate impose problems that at first glance might appear impossible to solve, but which fall apart when the experience of recent years and improvements in technology are applied. This does not mean that the solutions are simple. Planning must be detailed and done carefully, well in advance. Equipment should be chosen only after exhaustive study of the conditions under which it will be used. Consider transportation, for instance: a choice must be made between winter and summer; and there is the question of whether materials should be moved in bulk or be packaged. All these questions in their turn make the planning of the actual operation much more important.

Then the operation of the mine has to contend with the full, year-round cycle of the arctic climate. Installations must be so designed that the wind-chill effect of low temperatures along with high winds does not interfere. Men must be able to work in comfort in all conditions, in all seasons. The effect of very cold air on the operation of compressors and internal combustion engines must be considered. The impact of permafrost on the actual extraction must be allowed for. But conditions are not all adverse; there are a number of characteristics which are a decided advantage in mineral development, one of the most striking being the lack of vegetation — though in southern Canada this tends to hamper prospecting and geological mapping. In the short northern summer almost as much can be accomplished as in the longer southern summer.

Mines can be successfully operated even in the very high arctic, provided the men undertaking the project are completely familiar with the basic technology and can accurately assess the effect on the general and local arctic conditions. In short, "know your job." At present, there are individuals with arctic knowledge and experience; fortunately, for the arctic makes no concession to the human being or to southern civilization. It does not afford a second chance. The weak, the obstinate and the stupid are ruthlessly dealt with. But for those with the necessary determination, intelligence and ability to use the experience of others, the rewards are great, both spiritually and economically. Certainly the minerals are there. One of the world's largest deposits of iron ore is found on the Snake River in the northern Yukon. In northern Baffin Island, at Inuktorfik, a mountain of almost pure iron has been discovered. Over large parts of the arctic the glaciers have done an excellent job of stripping off the overburden above the ore bodies. With modern equipment such as airborne magnetometers, the task of locating and delineating the northern ore bodies is much simplified . . . the iron ore deposit at Inuktorfik was spotted from the air.

But the Canadian north is a vast country, the ore deposits are scattered and far from ports, and the climate is severe. The land itself sets the limits. While the chances of coming across a rich placer stream or a fabulous outcrop of mineral wealth are still there, thus adding excitement to the hunt for northern mineral wealth, its future development today depends on large-scale capitalization. The Iron Ore Company of Canada's initial operation in the heart of Labrador-Ungava cost half a billion dollars; International Nickel's Thompson operation cost even more. To go with this massive capital investment, northern mining development, along with a high level of science and technology, will also require the right sort of labour force. Otherwise these investments will just not pay. The Russians developed their northern mineral deposits on a vast scale, creating large cities like Noril'sk, with its 150,000 inhabitants. How? All the evidence points to the use of large numbers of slave labourers in the past to build the smelters, drive the shafts, and bring the mines into production. Because capital was short, they substituted brute force. Canada depends on a combination of heavy capital investment and advanced technology. Slave labour, even if it were available, is uneconomical over the long run.

Today the Russians' recruiting program lures skilled people north with a combination of high wages, good conditions and other lures. In our country the federal government has built roads, improved airstrips, developed harbours and provided tax relief and other incentives for northern companies, but the development of the mineral wealth still depends on the mining men and thus, one of the major concerns in northern mining must always be the well-being of the individual worker. He must be well paid, well trained, given plenty of responsibility and kept in efficient comfort, both on and off the job. Where in the past the pit foreman was the man with the loudest voice and the biggest fist, the men in charge of today's mining operations are skilled engineers and technologists. Any other form of labour is just too expensive. But as one resource expert noted, "Resources *are* not, they *become*."

Some of the Klondike gold-seekers followed the Mackenzie Valley route to the Yukon. On their way towards Great Slave Lake they noted large outcrops of silver-lead-zinc. They did not stop to stake or to mine, and nearly three-quarters of a century passed before the Pine Point deposits finally came into production. A railway, a massive mining operation, a power plant, and a town sprang up in a few years. From the prospector's pan to the giant shovel is a long way in the history of mining, but in Canada's north this development has been compressed into the life span of a man — a concrete example of what can, will and should be the future pattern of mining in the north.

WILLIAM M. GILCHRIST, *President, Eldorado Mining and Refining Ltd. Born Weyburn, Sask., 1909. B.Sc., Queens, 1936. War service R.C.E. Worked for northern mining companies in exploration and development in Northwest Territories. President, Northern Transportation Co. Ltd.; Director Eldorado Aviation Ltd.; Director Atomic Energy Control Board, Canadian Nuclear Association and The Mining Association of Canada. Member Advisory Panel of the Privy Council on Scientific and Industrial Research; Canadian Institute of Mining and Metallurgy; Arctic Institute of North America.*

DR. JACOB FRIED

Boom Towns . . . Must they Bust?

Our lack of knowledge on the whereabouts of
mineral deposits is partly responsible
for booms-to-bust towns. More research will
be necessary to prevent
the ups and downs of local economies.

Not long ago, I sat in a somewhat rickety cabin in Yellowknife and listened with mingled admiration and scepticism to yet another old timer tell me what was wrong with the far north. "Sonny," he said, "you can tie up the story of the north in three words: boom and bust."

The boom we were discussing was the vast post-war influx of federal government goods, services, and manpower which had changed the face of Yellowknife, so recently a boom-time mining community. The old timer with obvious relish, predicted that this boom too would "bust" just like all the others, because it was just natural that it should. This was a nasty habit of the region. He did not think that government enterprise would really settle the region down and tame it, because as he put it, "Where's the economics of it?" The sort of things that bring people into the region always seem to get used up. Between us, we made a list of booms and busts since the Yukon gold rush of the late 1890's. That boom brought in thousands of miners, transportation workers, and businessmen. Large towns like Whitehorse flourished. But just after the turn of the century, large corporate enterprises introduced a mechanized mode of production which rapidly made most of the population superfluous. Within a few short years, the swollen local population shrivelled away — boom and bust.

The 1920's, the time of the fur boom, brought considerable wealth to the inhabitants of the Yukon and Northwest Territories. This time it also benefited Indians and Eskimos, some of whom, as family trapping units, earned many thousands of dollars a year. Fur towns like Aklavik in the Mackenzie Delta area swelled with a polyglot population. It then had its short-lived classic period, if we may call it that. In the 1950's, its very existence was threatened and attempts were made to remove all its inhabitants to a new site, Inuvik. The fur-based economy was finished.

World War II brought the northern regions again economically to life, this time because of strategic consideration rather than some form of resource harvesting. A major supply route for oil and other military supplies for Alaska and the Asian theatre of war moved down the Mackenzie River and along a new highway route. Local transportation centres like Fort Smith and Whitehorse mushroomed in size, population and dollars. Similarly in the eastern arctic, Frobisher Bay, amidst the wastes of Baffin Island, became a vast military complex, one that drew hundreds of Eskimos into its orbit, and transformed them into townsmen.

Churchill, Manitoba, formerly a wintertime ghost town, which came to life only during the summer grain shipping season as a sea-port, became a military base around which a satellite town of skilled and unskilled workers grew, together with a large squatter population of Metis, Indians, and indigent whites. Of course, with the end of the war, this peculiar economic situation deteriorated immediately in some areas, though Fort Churchill until very recently was still active enough to support a boom town. Townsmen, dependent upon such an unreliable resource, naturally tend to get left stranded, like flotsam and jetsam on the beach after a violent storm, when there is a military pullback.

The effect of mining operations in the north since the last war, just as in the past, has not guaranteed the stability of northern town populations, even when it temporarily enriched them. Yellowknife is a fortunate community in that both the mining and government employment sectors supply fairly long-range economic stability. Elliot Lake, a mining community producing uranium ore, was not so fortunate, as both science and politics seemed bent on abandoning it. An even sadder case is that of Rankin Inlet, a nickel mining operation on the west coast of Hudson Bay which had successfully trained a large force of Eskimo miners, and then ran out of ore after a few short years of operation. And now, since the 1950's, large towns are again mushrooming in the north, based on a new type of resource. Inuvik, Fort Smith, and Frobisher Bay are complex government administrative centres established to foster and guide the varied programs of social and economic development of the region, and to integrate the native peoples into the body of national life. A new influx of transient and semi-transient people, the government civil servant foremost among these, came to join the earlier waves of highly mobile prospectors, miners, transportation workers, and fur traders. Thus, a history of the north can be written in terms of the specific resources — natural as in minerals or furs, non-natural as in strategic, welfare, or administrative national needs — which emerged one after another in the region. But all too often the resource has proved ephemeral.

Now, let us turn to a consideration of towns and town life under these conditions just sketched. The problems of northern development are not solely inherent in its frontier, rugged and isolated character, but in the inability of local as well as national agents and agencies to find a stable viable economy upon which to build communities. The difficulty does not lie entirely in this factor of instability alone, but also, in part, on the insistence of some community planners that modern town life in the north for both whites and natives be like the stable community life of the temperate heartland. Thus, we bend every effort in large towns to create impressive town settings, to build fine schools, churches, and homes all in the format of the temperate zone and this sometimes regardless of the lack of surrounding resources to support these facilities.

I found it personally refreshing to visit Aklavik, because there a northern style of life had at least temporarily evolved, developing this pattern out of years of living in the local natural setting. Today, many of its residents are still resisting efforts to change their ways and this they do not entirely out of orneriness. Though this life-style does not, in terms of standards of living, approach the level of southern living, it is nevertheless an authentic mode that emerged from the land and is rooted in local conditions. Aklavik stands in sharp contrast to the new town, Inuvik, which is rightly called a "piece of transplanted south." Under boom-time conditions, it is always possible to export the goods and services from the south to the north, whether it is champagne and grand pianos for the saloons of old Dawson, or hi-fi sets and suburban houses in modern Frobisher Bay; but under bust conditions, what can the region really support? Now all of these ups and downs need not necessarily have tragic consequences as long as the people involved are a specialized breed of adventurous miners, prospectors, oil-drillers, or well-paid and protected civil servants — men who are prepared to be mobile, who expect there to be an element of risk, and who only represent a selected and tiny segment of the total white Canadian society. But the Indians and Eskimos who are involved in these boom activities are not a tiny minority, but whole peoples whose destinies get linked to local and sometimes ephemeral outbursts of economic and political energy. Each time a resource fails, a resource based on some need or development in the southern regions, the local native population, who have lost their former traditional economic self-sufficiency, suffer.

The critical need is to recognize the economic limitations of the region in the present, and plan accordingly. Economic resources as related to our national economy are extremely localized in space at a few points where mines or transportation centres are to be found, and they may have an active economic life for a few short years. Also, as mining activities get more mechanized, the manpower needs can even conceivably shrink and not augment.

What kind of town-based communities should evolve to fit these local requirements? There is room in the north for communities like Aklavik where whites and natives, Indian and Eskimo, can preserve some local economy based at least in part on local resources such as furs or timber. There is also place for communities like Elliot Lake, Pine Point or Yellowknife with their specialized mining populations which are organized essentially along the same way as their counterparts farther south. The former populations survived the booms because somehow they were committed to the region, while the latter types, when they feel the pinch, fold their tents and drift on. There should be a clear distinction made between long-life or permanent communities, and planned short-life communities. They should not display different sorts of populations but vary considerably in their facilities.

DR. JACOB FRIED, *Professor, Department of Anthropology, Portland State College. Born Philadelphia, 1924. B.A., Temple University; Ph.D. in Anthropology, Yale. Field trips to Hawaii, Mexico, Peru, Canadian subarctic and arctic. Participated in Arctic Symposium at McGill, 1963. Chaired American Association for the Advancement of Science meetings in Montreal to discuss arctic problems, Montreal 1965. Associate Professor, Department of Anthropology, McGill 1962-65.*

PROF. FRANK VALLEE

The Co-operative Movement in the North

*The people of the north are slowly taking a
greater interest in their own affairs
and the development of their communities.
The co-operative movement, once
cut loose from overwhelming influence
from outside, can play an important role in
making the people think for themselves.*

One of the most significant developments among native peoples in Canada's arctic and subarctic during the past several years has been the establishment of co-operative societies in about 20 communities. The four governments with jurisdiction over most of the native peoples in the far north are: the federal government, the Quebec provincial government, and the governments of the Yukon and of the Northwest Territories. They support this development with specific programs aimed at raising living standards, and encouraging people to take a hand in running some of their own affairs.

There has been a steady rise in the level of wants among Eskimos and Indians. For instance, they want houses instead of tents. Houses have to be furnished, and in the far north, where wood is scarce, they have to be heated with very expensive oil. Not only household items and services, but other needs, such as clothing, food, radios, toys, are costlier in the north than in the south. While their wants have been rising there has been a steady decline in value or in pay-off from the traditional pursuits of hunting and trapping. Thus the gap between wants and income has been widening. This gap has been partly bridged by relief and other welfare payments, and by

ILLUSTRATIONS

29

30

31

34

35

36

37

38

39

40

41

42

43

44

45

46

47

wages earned in working for government or other institutions. This work is mostly casual and low skilled; few Indians or Eskimos have been able to take advantage of mining and other developments which have taken place on their own doorstep. There are several reasons for this; the chief one is lack of training, and experience in industrial occupations.

In many northern communities the wide gap between wants and the income needed to satisfy the wants calls for special arrangements, and the co-operative is such an arrangement. In the co-operative the members pool their efforts in the production of a wide variety of things for their own use and for outside markets. They are encouraged to exploit whatever there is to exploit in their regions: fish, seals, whales, lumber and so on. They are encouraged to develop their own human skills as well, and to produce carvings, garments, prints, and other objects for outside markets. People and agencies from the south who are interested in the northern co-operative movement assist by giving technical advice, and by providing grants and loans for liquid capital and plants needed by the local organization.

One should not exaggerate the economic significance of these hinterland co-operatives in the total picture. In a few communities, such as George River and Povungnituk in arctic Quebec, and Cape Dorset, Aklavik, and Fort Franklin in the Northwest Territories, substantial gains have been made in earned income through the local co-operatives. In these places relief payments have declined as more and more people are getting involved in production. In most places, however, where there are co-operatives, only a small number of people are reaping substantial economic benefits.

Let us look at the total picture for a moment. How many native people — that is, Eskimos, treaty Indians, non-treaty Indians and Metis — are there in arctic and subarctic Canada? There are over 20,000. Now my estimate is that only 4,000 of these native peoples have in their vicinities a co-operative which they can join as active participants. Thus, many thousands are outside the co-operative orbits. To raise the living standards for this considerable number, ways must be found to fit native peoples into the arctic industry developing all around them. Massive training and re-training programs will have to be instituted by government agencies in collaboration with mining, lumber, transportation, and tourist interests, as well as with unions, to channel native peoples into skilled jobs which in turn will fit into the developing northern economy.

However, such a program is not the topic of this article. I make the point only to put the economic aspects of northern co-operatives into perspective. The point is this: on the big economic scene, the co-operatives create more than a ripple but hardly a tidal wave. Cottage industry, wildlife harvesting, and art production are economically feasible activities here and there, and are best handled co-operatively, but in many places these are not economically feasible activities, in view of the steadily rising level of wants among native peoples. Although there is only limited economic value in far northern co-operatives, I believe they are still worth heavy support for their social and psychological value. Native peoples have had others making too many decisions for them. They have become socially and psychologically, as well as economically, dependent.

In a well-run co-operative the members take part in making decisions about what they are going to do, what they are going to borrow, lend, or what they are going to re-invest, distribute in profits, and the like. In a well-run co-operative the local people provide the working force, the managers, book-keepers, shippers, janitors, salesmen, etc. In the far north, the co-operatives are a training ground for people, in what to them have appeared as occult arts and skills. I cannot stress strongly enough the adult educational value of far northern co-operatives; even if they made no money at all, I would strongly support the movement because of its educational and emancipating consequences. These consequences are evident in those few far northern co-operatives which have several different kinds of operation under their control. The one I know best, the Povungnituk Co-operative Society in arctic Quebec, has a carving branch, a print shop, a fishing branch, a sewing branch for garments, a tourist branch, a modern store, and a credit union which is really the local bank. Each branch or operation has policy committees, its own working staff, and its own managerial staff. Committees and staff are about 98 per cent Eskimo. It would be hard to estimate the adult educational value of this enterprise, but it is considerable. A multi-purpose co-operative like this one becomes something akin to a local government in the community making decisions about community affairs which in reality have nothing to do with the co-operative. Co-operatives such as this have a maximum community impact. Unfortunately, most far northern co-operatives are not like this, most have only one or two operations under their control like marketing or housing or fishing, and have only a limited impact on the community as a whole.

Multi-purpose and single-purpose co-operatives in the far north may differ in their significance for the community, but they do have one thing in common, they all follow a certain pattern of establishment and development. All have been founded or instigated by persons from outside, non-natives. In most cases these have been members of the industrial division of the department of northern affairs, which has a separate co-operative section. But others from outside the federal government have been instigators too. The Oblate Order has no special program and yet four of its missionaries have launched co-operatives in their communities. In another place a co-operative development officer hired by the Co-operative Union of Canada has been the instigator and is working under contract for the Northwest Territories Council.

All of these outsiders, governmental and otherwise, have bucked serious impediments in getting their operations going. They have all come through periods when it looked as though the operation was going to fold for lack of internal and external support. They deal with people who are not accustomed to making decisions about their economic and social welfare on a community-wide basis; they deal with people who say, "Well, this is just another gimmick of the white man to keep us in our place." They deal with people who are impatient with talk, talk, talk, and who evaluate things by their results; they deal with people in communities that are frequently divided into factions, Protestant and Catholic, Metis and Indian, Eskimo and Indian. In short, these are places where there is not much precedent for co-operation cutting across the whole community.

In overcoming these impediments, the outside instigators have had the support of native enthusiasts in their communities. In almost all of the communities where co-operatives have been established, you will find a small nucleus of native people who become converted to the co-operative ideology. They are typically young adults between the age of 25 to 40 years, people who would not have been leaders in traditional times. These are people whose skills are suited to the present. They are flexible and they try to learn the ropes of modern life. This does not mean that they become less Indian or Eskimo in their feelings; some of these native co-operative leaders are strongly nationalistic or nativistic, and want to work loose from white control. This latter point takes on special significance when we consider that the arctic and subarctic co-operatives provide one of the few channels along which native people can link up with others like them outside their own communities. The movement could be a vehicle for a pan-Eskimo, pan-Indian expression of voice, and that, I submit, is one thing we need in this country.

To sum up, I am an enthusiastic supporter of the co-operative movement in the arctic and subarctic regions of Canada, not so much because of the economic value of the co-operative, although this is considerable, but more because of its social and psychological value in helping people work away from the disheartening, demoralizing status they had in the past, when they looked for their signals from government officials, traders, police and missionaries.

PROFESSOR FRANK VALLEE, *Professor of Sociology, Carleton University, Ottawa. Born Montreal, 1918. B.A. (Hons.), McGill University, 1950; Ph.D., London, England, 1955. Lectured University of Edinburgh and McMaster University, Hamilton. Chief of Research Division, Dept. of Citizenship and Immigration, 1955-57. Arctic research in District of Keewatin, area of Baker Lake, eastern arctic, southern Baffin Island and Ungava Bay.*

H. J. WILLIAMSON

From Shaman's Flight
to Satellite

*Not so long ago the Indians were skeptical
of the white man's strange notions about
communications. But the vast expenditures that
followed each communications break-through
have produced results which far
surpass the Shaman's fantasies.*

We can go back as far as 1850 when plans, which were later abandoned, provided a telegraph line to link the western United States
through the Yukon, with Russia and thence to Europe in case a
trans-Atlantic telegraph cable failed, but another cable superseded,
and the overland route was never completed. However, in 1898-99
the latest strikes at Bonanza or Hunker Creek and on the Klondike
saw a telegraph line, from Dawson city to Lake Bennett, joined to
the wires of the White Pass Railway to Skagway. In 1901 the Lake
Bennett end of the Dawson line was extended to Atlin, then through
Telegraph Creek, on to Hazleton and south through the Cariboo
country to Vancouver and Seattle. This line, later known as the
Government Telegraph Service, with radio to replace sections which
couldn't be kept in repair, operated until about 15 years ago when
it was replaced by modern and more reliable services.

In 1923, Dawson and Mayo Landing were connected by Royal
Canadian Corps of Signals stations, as the first points of what later
became the N.W.T. and Y. of the R.C.C.S. This proud and historical
agency could write many chapters on its role in tying the Canadian
north together. It was the sinew of this communications network
that, as much as any other single force, rolled back our northern

frontiers. Plans to develop a station at Herschel Island seemed to be doomed. Aklavik was one of the next jewels to be added to the chain, along with Edmonton. This was the base station and nerve centre of the developing system which in the next ten years saw all the then major communities of the Canadian north tied together. A single station of the department of marine, later department of transport, at Coppermine, came on to the scene in 1930-31. In the east, about the same time, communications were limited to the Hudson Strait and Hudson Bay as far north as Chesterfield Inlet. Marine Direction Finding Stations in isolated inland points were linked together using old spark-type transmitters. Port Nelson and later Churchill became western focal points, in addition to connections they had with their headquarters in Ottawa.

Increased use of the aeroplane saw radio equipment take to the air. The increase of communications with stations was gradually established by the owners of the aircraft, but more often with the Royal Canadian Corps of Signals or the Hudson's Bay post. That company decided in 1934 to use radio, mostly in code at first. Wolstenholme in the eastern Hudson Strait area was the Bay's first station to open.

World War II brought about the North West Staging Route (N.W.S.R.) through the Yukon to Alaska, with an alternate route through or via Dawson city. Then came the feverish activity of the Canol Project and what it did to the Mackenzie as far as Norman Wells and the Imperial Oil exploration beyond. With mining at Yellowknife and Port Radium, expanding air activity, the need for Radio Aids to Navigation and more weather reports, communications hummed.

The post-war years saw military installations transformed to civilian needs. Joint Arctic Weather Stations were built and then arose the necessity for connections with regular and reliable networks to the weather circuits of the world. The DEW Line followed with all its feverish activity and the development of its myriad of complex radars and communications.

For years the Canadian Broadcasting Corporation, through its Northern Service, has beamed special programs to the north. This medium continues to serve many of the isolated communities, small groups of people, and the lone individual. 'Till radio came into being, their only means of communication with the "outside" had been a once-a-year-mail delivery. This radio service which in many instances is an outgrowth of military establishments continues to grow as an outpost of the national radio system.

So coming to the present an inventory of the changes shows that with modern transistorized radio receivers, more powerful broadcasting stations, tape recorders with voices on tape from home by more frequent mail, telephones, teletypes, two-way radio to talk to neighbours or in some instances to the foreman or head office all adds up to almost Utopia. Compared with the old days, the arctic seems to be literally over-run with all kinds of activity, and people and things are, to say the least, different.

The Royal Canadian Corps of Signals have gone and they have been missed. The Bay now runs upwards of 80 radio stations and at one time their number passed the hundred mark. The R.C.M.P. have radio at most of their detachments. The D.O.T. is here, there and everywhere: on airports, weather stations, on ice-breakers, and ships. The national health and welfare hospitals and nursing stations are getting more radio facilities. Northern affairs have their sets. Northern Transportation has radio on its tugs and barges. Oil and mining explorations have their Single Side Band units. Canadian National Telecommunications and the Bell Telephone Company are providing base station facilities for many of these radios. They provide not only local telephone exchange services, but connection by radio or wire line to the communications networks of the continent and the world.

Because of the wire line or micro-wave circuits either paralleling or leapfrogging them many of the communities in the western arctic mainland, from Cambridge Bay westward, have local telephone exchanges and quite a few of them have access to line communications with the outside. The latest link in this chain is the wire line system, provided by Canadian National Telecommunications, extending down the Mackenzie. This has linked places like Fort Simpson, Wrigley, Fort Norman, Norman Wells, Fort Good Hope and Inuvik to the southern part of our country. Limited communications and the uncertainty of radio circuits are replaced by a modern and more positive service. It marks at the same time the end and the beginning of an era. In the eastern arctic, however, that old salt water that stays frozen most of the year makes construction a bit different. While many communities have local telephone service, the long distance connections rely on radio, which can be very good,

62015

51

but unfortunately not always is. The Bell Telephone Company is looking forward to the day when the volume of business increases. Then they will be able to replace the well-worth pioneer circuits with a new type using improved technology, which is more reliable.

Who would have thought as little as ten years ago that you could roll off the following places as a list of telephone exchanges in the far north — Resolute Bay, Pond Inlet, Igloolik, Arctic Bay, Cambridge Bay, Inuvik, Aklavik and further south but still well in the north at Dawson, Norman Wells, Baker Lake, Eskimo Point, Chesterfield Inlet, Frobisher Bay, Pangnirtung, and many others coming in the very near future. So much for telephones.

The Joint Arctic Weather Station sites serve as advance bases for high arctic explorations. Advance units have set up their camps and radio facilities near the weather station, and they direct operations over a large radius. The weather stations and their communications also stand as ears for Air Traffic Control positions. They report the whereabouts of jet commercial aircraft that whistle through the narrow time zones on the polar route from Europe to the far east. This information is funnelled to control stations in Anchorage and Goose Bay to fit into the terminal traffic patterns as they are relayed around the world.

Two other special communication functions are related to these weather stations. Radiosonde, with automatic signals received from small battery-operated transmitters in high-flying weather balloons, is used to record temperature, humidity, and barometric pressure, and from tracking information, wind velocities. This information has to be relayed to the south to join the weather circuits of the world. In return, the south sends back by radio, maps of the total area weather conditions by a photo-electric scanning process to Resolute Bay, the most southern of the Joint Arctic Weather Stations in our north. These weather charts can also be copied by ships, particularly by the ice-breakers which convoy the supply fleet each summer — special communications indeed.

What of the future? My crystal ball is clouded, but the services I have already mentioned will increase and expand, and believe it or not, considerable thought and money is being spent on a feasibility study to cover the North American continent with TV from satellites. This would include possible viewing as far north as 70 degrees or further. These same satellites might also be used as paths for telephone circuits from north to south, and they would not be any more expensive than if provided on a lightly loaded tropo-scatter system, but definitely more reliable than present day high frequency radio even in the Single Side Band mode.

Some communities could now have closed circuit TV, but it would be costly. However, if the progress in the next 35 years matches that of those just past, these and stranger things may happen. But right now I wouldn't recommend our northerners rushing to the Bay or sending a mail order outside for a TV set. Who knows, though, the next generation might well, with apologies to Robert Service, chant —

> The Northern Lights have seen queer sights,
> But it's now not so strange to see,
> When on the marge of Lake LeBarge,
> A spaceman on Coloured TV.

H. J. WILLIAMSON, *Chief of Technical and Policy Co-ordination, Department of Transport. Born Regina, 1909. Degree in Electrical Engineering, University of New Brunswick, 1930. Career mainly concerned with telecommunications for Department of Transport in several areas in Canada including Arctic Islands. Head of Canadian delegation to Geneva dealing with telecommunications problems, 1963 and 1964. Responsible for construction of Canadian Satellite Communications Station at Mill Village where Canadian participation in Early Bird and future communications satellites will be centred.*

W. E. BROWN

. . . and How to Get From
Point to Point

*Travel in the north can still be challenging
and if one uses dogteams it will most
certainly be an experience. How do the dogs
feel about it? Well, that seems
to depend on the type of harness used.*

Transportation may now be the largest single industry in southern Canada, but it has developed very slowly in our arctic and subarctic areas. The reason lies with the pure and simple economics of the problem.

We are apt to regard overland transportation as comparatively simple . . . *anything* can be moved *anywhere*, providing cost is no object. However, in the north cost is a very real problem. This territory, comprising almost two-thirds of Canada's three and a half million square miles of land, is almost devoid of railways and access roads. The short summer and the long, harsh winter season, plus one-way cargoes, make overland transportation a very costly business. High freight rates mean higher living costs, and this in an area where the average *per capita* annual income is the lowest in Canada.

As late as 1920 this vast land could only be reached by one of three routes: down the rivers flowing into the Arctic Ocean or Hudson Bay, by ship from the Pacific Coast to a few distributing points in the western arctic, or by ship from Atlantic ports through Hudson Strait into Hudson and James Bay. Due to these transport restrictions, the few small settlements were built along the more or less navigable rivers which, depending on the season, were the highways of the north, or along the accessible part of the coast. The greatest problem was the distribution of supplies to inland points and, until recent years, this could only be carried out by very primitive means.

Winter is the most important season in the north, because it's by far the longest. During that period the dogteam was the main form of transport and is still used by some trappers. Among dog-team buffs there are as many models of sleds and toboggans as there are automobile models on today's car lots. These vary from the elaborate basket sled of Alaska and the Yukon, or the jumper sled of northern British Columbia, to the widely-used toboggan of the northern Indians east of the Rocky Mountains, and the komatik of the Eskimos. Types of harnesses and dogs are equally varied. Each sled model has been developed to meet local conditions, although on one occasion I had serious doubts on that score. During the course of an inspection trip some years ago, through the Cassiar country of northern British Columbia, I spent many days travelling by dogteam. Jumper sleds were used, a type designed for crusted snow. But unfortunately that's not what we ran into, and we almost bogged down in soft, deep snow — a condition that calls for a toboggan-type of hand or dog sled.

The toboggan type is the most widely used of all. Originally hand-hewn, usually from birch, the modern one is now generally constructed of oak. It is made of two eight-inch-wide boards, giving the toboggan a total width of 16 inches. Pre-bent to shape, it has a very high curved head, which makes it well adapted for negotiating narrow bush trails. The length, or "drag" is based on the length of the board's actual contact with the snow, not including the head, and this can vary from a six- to a 16-foot drag.

The modern Eskimo sled, or komatik, is usually made from sitka spruce and varies in length from 10 feet to 24 feet, although, in the Ashiarmuit country I have seen 30-feet long komatiks made from spliced, local black spruce. These sleds are built on two runners fastened together with crossbars lashed across the top. Metal is never used as a fastening as it becomes too brittle in low temperatures. With all the white man's technological progress, it is doubtful that we can show an Eskimo a more friction-free surface than the mudded sled runner. The process of "mudding" a sled is very like a child's mud-pie making technique. The exception is that the mud is moulded on the bottom of the runner, carefully planed down to a smooth surface, and iced. This icing process is carried out by filling the mouth with water and squirting it on a small piece of polar bearskin held in the hand. This water-saturated bearskin is rubbed back and forth on the mud surface, leaving a thin film of ice. The secret of a good running surface is complete coverage with the thinnest possible film of ice. Part of an Eskimo's trail equipment is a small bag of earth, a piece of bearskin, and a small, often home-made, plane. Earth is not too plentiful in the Barrens and, in travelling over rocky terrain, the spare earth supply can be exhausted at times. On several trips I've made, it's been necessary to use flour or rolled oats, taken from our precious food supply, to replace the mud lost off the komatik. With a freshly-iced sled it's possible to move a 1,200-pound load on level snow, with one hand.

Types of harnesses and hitches are almost as varied as the sleds. But, after travelling many thousands of miles by dog sled, through all sections of the Canadian arctic and subarctic, I'd class the Eskimo harness as the most efficient; in fact if I were a sled dog, with free choice, that's the type I would choose without hesitation. The dogs are hitched to the toboggan in tandem, with leather traces and leather collars. This is different from the Alaskan hitch of two dogs abreast on a single trace, with one leader in front. I should also mention that the dogs differ widely in the north, with the Eskimo dog of the eastern arctic a heavier, slower type than the rangier dogs of the Mackenzie and Yukon areas.

During the few short summer months the Eskimo, until recently, was often forced to pack his supplies on his own back, or on the backs of his dogs, when moving from the coast to his inland trapping camp. On the other hand, the Indian did most of his travelling and hauling of supplies by canoe. These early craft were made of birch-bark and were a miracle of lightness. However, they were easily damaged and, on that account, were replaced by the conventional canvas-covered canoe.

With the expanding economy of the north, and the development of the internal combustion engine, efforts were directed towards using this source of energy to reduce the costs of overland transport. Outboard motors took over a good share of the work of native paddlers, just as motor toboggans and ski-doos are now fast replac-

ing the dogteam. Tractor trains handle much of the freight once
brought to subarctic trading posts by canoe, dogteam and horse
toboggan. But in the final analysis, it has been the aeroplane which
has supplied the answer to the problem of overland transportation
in the arctic. Flights were made into the north as early as 1921.
There was the famed Imperial Oil flight into Fort Norman, the local
manufacture of propellers out of sled boards and home-made
moosehide glue, the story-book adventure of the two Junkers and
pilots Gorman and Fullerton. But it was not until 1928 that the
aeroplane came into its own in the Canadian north. In that year,
a sudden flurry of prospecting activity took place in the Northwest
Territories and the Eskimos, for the first time, were able to marvel
at the "Tingmishoot" or big bird. From the village's oldest patriarch
to the youngest child, everyone was eager to ride in the planes, but
there was also some hard-headed thinking about them. For example,
I can remember the arrival of one of the first planes at Chesterfield
Inlet. It was a Fairchild 71, piloted by Matt Berry, of Northern
Aerial Mineral Explorations. The plane was hauled up on the beach
and we were helping the pilot to "gas up" the machine. One of the
Eskimo elders, known as "Black Peter," a nickname that had survived from his whaling days, surveyed it from all angles. After his
exhaustive inspection, he came over to us. "That," he said, pointing
to the plane, "is a bad thing to know just a little bit about."

Great credit is due to those pioneer pilots who first penetrated
the arctic wastelands, at great personal risk and under extremely
difficult conditions — Pat Reid, Jimmy Vance, Bill Spence, Captain
Sutton, men who later died in the wreckage of aircraft. Then there
were Wop May, Roy Brown, Matt Berry, Duke Schiller, to name
but a few who blazed the skyways when the north had nothing to
offer the navigator other than unending, empty space. Today the
arctic and subarctic regions are dotted with landing fields for use
by the multi-engine aircraft. Weather stations and radio communications contribute their share towards the safety of arctic flying
while, in the far north, the probing radars of the DEW Line add
their final note of security to the transport planes which shuttle back
and forth over that great lone land.

In northern Canada the York boat has ceased to exist. Kayaks
and umiaks are almost lost in memory. Dogteam and canoe travel
are fast fading out of the picture. In view of the recent major changes

in our overland transport system, one cannot help but wonder what, in the future, will supersede the aeroplane.

W. E. BROWN, *Transport Manager, Hudson's Bay Company, Winnipeg. Born Vancouver. Arctic service with R.C.M.P. Forty years with Hudson's Bay Company. Company positions at Eskimo Point, James Bay, Mackenzie River and Nelson River. Established tractor route from Wager Inlet to Chantrey Inlet, supervised transport from Fort Norman to Echo Bay, survey of fur trade potential on Pacific Coast and Alaska. Speaks Eskimo.*

COMMODORE O. S. C. ROBERTSON

The Canadian Arctic
Water Basin

The shape of ships plying the
Northwest Passage in years to come will
probably be a far cry from Henry Larsen's
St. Roch, the first ship to
make a successful crossing, 1941-43.

Transportation by water into and through the arctic is expensive
and difficult. The nature of the terrain, the persistence of sea-ice
and the climate are the limiting factors. Until recently, because of
these restrictions, very few people travelled to this region for pleasure
or for profit. The last decade though has seen new vehicles and
techniques developed which can operate successfully within the
arctic environment. The cost of development, production and
operation is much higher than for similar operations in more temperate climates. Some of these higher costs are undoubtedly due
to the relatively small size of existing operations. The degree to
which all this is true varies with the geography, and what holds for
one area may not be right or may even be completely wrong in
another area. The greatest tonnage transported into and through
the area is carried by surface sea carriers.

Shipping in the North American Arctic Basin can be divided into
two sections and they are quite different kettles of fish. It is possible
to ship from the Atlantic to the Pacific, or vice versa, through the
Northwest Passage, but this cannot be considered a commercially
sound practice. The shipping season itself is too short and, for
conventional shipping, there are too many dangers. Shipping normally enters the western North American Arctic Basin through the

Bering Strait, along the north Alaskan coast, through the Beaufort Sea, Amundsen Gulf, Dolphin and Union Strait, Coronation Gulf, Dease Strait, Queen Maud Gulf, and Simpson Strait as far as Shepherd's Bay. This route is tortuous, only partially surveyed, and the limiting draft is about 25 feet. The ports served are Point Barrow, Barter Island, Tuktoyaktuk and Cambridge Bay, together with many small loading and unloading stations such as trading posts, R.C.M.P. posts, and missions, which could hardly be classified as ports. All cargo operations are over-the-beach type, with the exception of those at Tuktoyaktuk, where good wharfage is available. Unfortunately, while there is deep water in the harbour itself, a bar imposes a limited draft of about 14 feet at the entrance.

Tuktoyaktuk is the main trans-shipment point for goods coming down the Mackenzie River, the only south-north flowing river in North America which is both navigable and connected with the transportation system of the interior. Ocean shipping, unfortunately, cannot use this river because of the shallow delta at its mouth. Unlike the Soviet rivers, it is used to support the northern posts rather than to export the raw resources of the hinterland. The navigation season along this route extends from about the first week of August to about the third week of September, when west winds generally bring the polar pack down on the coast of Alaska, with Point Barrow receiving the first impact. This point acts as a fulcrum for the polar ice, and is the limiting factor in getting the ships in and out before the ice again descends on Point Barrow. In many years, the easterly winds commencing in early October take the pack off the coast again; this will allow shipping to round Point Barrow southbound, lengthening the season by two or three weeks. However, waiting for these easterly winds can be risky business. If they do not materialize, shipping is trapped for the winter as, in all probability, it would be too late to traverse the long run back to Shepherd Bay, through Barrow Strait, to the passages leading to the Atlantic. This escape route, if it is to be used at all, should be attempted in the late days of September or certainly no later than early October, and only then when seasonable winds bring the polar pack down on the northern Alaskan coast much earlier than usual.

In contrast to the western portion of the North American Arctic Basin, the eastern half presents, with the exception of the ice in the "Middle Pack" in Baffin Bay, less difficult conditions. The waters are deeper, the land bolder, and the hydrographic surveys, while nowhere approaching accuracy, do give some aid to the navigator. The main ports either have wharfage or a reasonable draft — about 28 feet — with good beaches, and a shipping season from the middle of May to late October. Frobisher Bay, with limited draft wharfage, has a shipping season from early August to early October; Churchill, on Hudson Bay, has good wharfage and a season that runs from the middle of July to late October. Thule, again with fine wharfage, from the middle of July to the middle of October; Resolute Bay, with adequate lighterage, is open from early August to late September. While other ports, such as Hall Lake, do not have wharfage or established lighterage, they are of sufficient size and importance. Unlike many of the western arctic ports, they do have in most cases adequate beaches, many of them man-made, hardstands, and adequate road systems to clear cargo from the beach area.

Again, unlike the Russian Northern Sea Route ports, the North American arctic ports are built to receive cargo and not for the export of cargo. The only exception is Churchill, which is one of our main export ports. Up to 70 ships call at Churchill during the shipping season, and carry away some 20 to 30 million bushels of wheat. There is also quite an inter-port cargo distribution from Churchill to the small ports of Eskimo Point, Chesterfield Inlet, and Rankin Inlet, on the west coast of Hudson Bay.

The Canadian-American Joint Weather Stations in the Queen Elizabeth Islands are in the main supplied by airlift, except Eureka, on the west coast of Ellesmere Island, which is supplied by large ice-breaking cargo ships. For some years, ice-breakers were used to re-supply weather and research stations on the Northern Waterway, that strip of water separating Greenland and Ellesmere Island, but now annual re-supply is carried out by airlift. The ice-breakers employed in the western North American Arctic Basin are supplied by the U.S. Navy and the U.S. Coast Guard — they are of the "Wind" class, about 6,000 tons and 1,200 horsepower. The Canadian Coast Guard operates one smaller ice-breaker in the Canadian sector. In the eastern North American Arctic Basin, the Americans have two or three "Wind" class ice-breakers, while the Canadians employ a fleet of some 10 ice-breakers of various classes. Some of these, the larger ones, like the *Sir John A. Macdonald,* and the *d'Iberville,* are ice-breaking cargo ships. They possess all the capability of an ice-breaker, and have good cargo capacity as well. In this section of the arctic, Danes, Americans and Canadians operate a number of ships that are "ice-strengthened." The Danish Lauretzen lines have the "Dan" class: the *Helgadan,* the *Manjadan* and several more, all ice-strengthened. The Americans have LSD's *Point Barrow* and *Lindenwald* and the U.S. "Altanin" and "Eltana" class which are cargo ships and tankers. The Canadian Coast Guard, many of whose ships are ice-strengthened, operates a large number for re-supply to Canadian northern sites, probably the best known being their Eastern Arctic Patrol ship, the *C. D. Howe.*

While nuclear submarines have not been used as commercial cargo carriers, it might be a good thing to take a quick look at their present capability. They can, as the United States and the U.S.S.R. navies have demonstrated in the last several years, operate in ice-covered or ice-infested waters during any season of the year, and traverse very shallow water avoiding ice of prohibitive draft. They have special sonar equipment which is used to guide the submarines past ice obstacles, and safely bring them to the surface through the ice-cover. The techniques which they use are now sufficiently developed and a submarine can, with certainty, navigate anywhere where the water is deep enough. They can detect ice ahead, and can either avoid icebergs or go underneath them if they are not too deep. They can do everything we want them to do — except carry enough cargo.

Improvements in instruments and techniques are constantly being sought and achieved. I suppose it's only fair to assume that arctic submarines will continue to improve through advanced submarine hull design, more efficient and less costly reactors, more sophisticated sonar equipment, and an increasing knowledge of arctic waters. The arctic submarine of today can transport men and very limited amounts of material to any ice-covered area which has sufficient sea-room under the ice-cover to permit submarine operations. Greater knowledge of local ice conditions and of water depths is necessary to effect exchange with beach or port activity. This knowledge is relatively easy to procure. The existing method of using the bubbler system can keep a harbour or docking area free of ice, as long as there is sufficient influx of underlying seawater at appropriate rates of salinity and temperature. Standard oceanographic observation will establish these facts. As more exact knowledge is obtained on the nature of sea ice, improvements will be made in the design of the hull, and in propulsion plants, both for surface and submarine cargo carriers.

Unfortunately, ships are built to last for about 20 to 30 years, or longer, and therefore improvements in hull configuration are slow to become apparent. Recent research in the physics of sea ice leads the naval architect to believe that vast improvements can be made in the design of ice-breakers intended for ice-escort work. I mean things like the beam-length ratio, bow structure, entry forms, etc.

Similarly, greater knowledge of ice behaviour and ice-working operations have shown that ice-strengthened ships can carry out tasks formerly reserved for ice-breakers. But the difference in cost between the ice-breaker and the ice-strengthened ship is formidable. Any decrease in the cost of shipping will help to open up our arctic littoral. With increasing knowledge of ice behaviour comes increased capability of conventional shipping in ice-infested waters. While the cost of nuclear submarine cargo carriers may be prohibitive except for low cube, high density, very valuable cargoes, thought might well be given to the design and operations of a nuclear submarine tug where homogeneous-type cargoes are pulled in dumb, simply constructed submarine barges. The advancement in marine cargo carriage methods and terminal handling of such cargo in arctic waters only awaits the demand for development. Many of the basic factors are now known and others are but waiting to be discovered.

COMMODORE O. S. C. ROBERTSON, *(Rtd.) Scientific Advisor to Canadian Corporation, 1967 World Exhibition. Born Victoria, B.C., 1907. George Medal. Commanded H.M.C.S. Labrador on maiden voyage circumnavigating North America and through Northwest Passage. Advisor on Seadragon through Northwest Passage and to North Pole, 1960. B.Sc., McGill University, 1963. Back Grant from Royal Geographical Society and Massey Medal. Fellow and past Governor, Arctic Institute of North America.*

COMMODORE O. S. C. ROBERTSON

The Russian Arctic
Water Basin

Because of some unpopularity quite a
while ago, the U.S.S.R. developed a Northern
Sea Route which today demands respect.
With the discovery of new minerals
and new ice-breakers it is still worthwhile.

The most efficient form of marine transportation systems at present
used in the arctic is undoubtedly the Soviet Northern Sea Route.
It consists of the Barents Sea to the Kara Sea. There are three straits
connecting these which can be used: the Matochkin Strait, the
Karskiya Vorota and the most southern one, the Ugorskiy Shar.
When the weather is very favourable the most northern route can be
used north of Novaya Zemlya and south of Franz Josef Island passing Cap Zhelaniya. From the Kara to the Laptev Sea the route goes
through the Vilkitskogo Strait; from the Laptev Sea through the
Dmitriya Lapteva Strait through the New Siberian Islands to the
Eastern Siberian Sea; from this sea through Strait Longa south of
Wrangel Island to the Chukchee Sea through Bering Strait to the port
of Provideniya. This route has opened lines of communication to
the interior of the eastern U.S.S.R., and has made possible the
exploitation of the raw resources of this area. It has halved the
distance between the Soviet European ports and the ports of the
Soviet far east.

Now why did the Soviets open up this route? Here we must go
back into history. In 1917 the Soviet government was not very
popular in the world. Very few nations would trade with her and
she therefore had to develop, within her own territories, the sources

of raw material she required. This was done in three ways. First of all, regrettably, the government drew on forced labour (to us, concentration camps). The second method, which came into effect after the concentration camps passed out of existence, was to entice people to move to the northern areas because it was needed by Mother Russia. It was a source of national pride to work in northern areas. Today this is no longer so, or not to the same extent. People work in the Soviet arctic because it is a good place to work, with the same facilities they have in other areas of the Soviet Republics.

Now while the Barents Sea is open all year round for conventional shipping, the other areas of the Northern Sea Route are without water transportation most of the year because of ice. Conventionally built ships can operate most years in the Kara Sea between late July and early October, in the Laptev Sea from about mid-July to early October, in the East Siberian Sea from late July to late September, and in the Bering Sea from early July to early October. However, by employing ice-breakers, as ice escorts and ice-working ships on the route, the navigation season has been extended anywhere from one to two months.

The U.S.S.R. has paid a great deal of attention to the development of this sea route, and we might ask ourselves why? For it would now appear that the north, except in the case of a few commodities, is not of particular importance to the Soviet economy as a whole. The area served by the Northern Sea Route has a population of approximately 5,000,000 people. Two of its cities, Archangel and Murmansk, have populations of approximately a quarter of a million each, and at least eight other cities have populations ranging from 60,000 to 100,000. Some contributions of the area are, however, significant: 35 per cent of the Soviet fish catch is caught in these waters, and 15 per cent of the timber is cut here, while 15 per cent of the copper, 80 per cent of the phosphates, 60 per cent of the cobalt nickel, and 40 per cent of the nation's tin are mined here. In addition, there are vast areas of potential wealth in gas, oil, and coal which, when exploited, will be served to some extent by this route.

In 1960 some 270 ships plied these waters carrying over a million tons of cargo. Most of these ships were between 2,500 tons and 3,500 tons, though some were of the 6,000 ton class or better. The size of ships is restricted due to the shallowness of the route, and this, of course, affects the tonnage. The limiting draft to which a ship can go is somewhere between 20 and 25 feet. The key to arctic shipping is the use of ice-breakers working in conjunction with ice-observation aircraft. Again in 1960, two important additions were made to the Russian ice-breaking fleet; the atomic-powered *Lenin,* she's some 16 thousand tons displacement and 44 thousand tons horsepower, and the Finnish-built diesel-electric *Moskva,* she's about 12 to 13 thousand tons with about 22 thousand tons horsepower. These operated throughout the season with eight other ice-breakers of more than 5,000 tons displacement: three of the "Stalin" class — that's the old name, I don't know what the new name is — the *Joseph Stalin,* the *Makanov,* and the *Lazarev;* three of the "Kapitan" class, the *Belousov,* the *Veronir*, and the *Melekhov;* the *Krasin;* and that grand old veteran, the *Yermak* — she was built in 1898 in Newcastle, and she's still a very fine ice-breaker. In addition there's a large fleet of ice-breaking tugs.

Many of the ships employed on this trade are ice-strengthened; that is, they're capable of independent movement in all but the heaviest of ice. Perhaps the best example of this type of ship is the "Lena" class; they were built in the Netherlands between 1954 and 1957, and have a cargo capacity of approximately 6,500 tons. It is understood from the best information I can get, that in addition to these six Dutch built ships, many others of the same class have been constructed in the U.S.S.R. itself.

One of the biggest factors in the success of this transportation complex is the large pool of very experienced ice-breaker officers and men, some with better than 30 years' experience in this class of ship. They have numerous aids to navigation along these routes, fueling stations, and excellent ice and weather reporting. The main ice-breaker stations are at Novaya Zemlya in the Siberian Islands, Wrangel Island, Provideniya, Borisa Vil Strait and in the Bering Strait.

The ports served by the northern sea lie principally at the mouths of the south-north flowing rivers, and near the major straits. The Soviets have to compete with an entirely different situation from what we have in North America. They have many south-north flowing rivers. Canada has only one which is navigable, the Mackenzie. The treeline in most cases in the Soviet arctic reaches the sea-coast.

In Canada, it extends to the sea in only one place, at the mouth of the Mackenzie. The river ports of the U.S.S.R. serve as trans-shipment points for the cargo bound in and out of the interior. The main terminal points are Archangel and Murmansk in the west, Petropaolosk-Kamshabski, Magadan, Uzhno-Sakahalinsk, and Vladivostok in the east. The main intermediate ports are Amderma, Dickson, Dudinka, Igarka, Tiksi, etc., most of which have alongside berthing. They have wharves which we don't have in the North American arctic. It is really a completely different problem, as comparison with the previous chapter shows. The Soviet ports on the Northern Sea Route are mainly geared to export, while the arctic ports of North America are mainly geared to import, with little or no export trade.

PROF. JIM LOTZ

The North as a Laboratory

*Day by day more mysteries of the north are
being unravelled, with benefits to north
and south alike. The whole pace of northern
development depends mainly on the sort
of questions scientists raise in the first place . . .
and then upon the use that is made of
the answers they obtain.*

Science, like love, cannot and perhaps should not be defined too precisely. It is very easy to describe what scientists do, but this in itself does not constitute science. Science perhaps can best be defined as problem-solving: asking questions and seeking answers.

In the north, the land beyond the treeline, you will find scientists scanning the skies and recording the changing patterns of the auroras. You will find them talking to Eskimos, recording their legends and asking them about their attitude towards wage employment. You will find them recording the growth rate of arctic char in lonely snow-fed lakes, watching and recording the slow seaward creep of glaciers, sending aloft balloons to measure the temperature of the air above the surface.

What the scientist does and where he does it depends on his training, his ability, his inclinations and his equipment. The north, as all who live there know, is a demanding place. The scientist, like other northern residents, frequently finds himself uncomfortable, but, unlike other northerners, he is seldom bored. For the north is a scientific frontier, and it is on the frontiers of the world and on the frontiers of knowledge that the interesting things happen, can be observed, and perhaps be understood. This is the primary appeal of the north to the scientist.

The work the scientist does in the north, remote from the settled parts of the world, may affect the health, happiness and comfort of everyone living south of the treeline. A storm that ravages the United States was born in part because of the movements of air masses in arctic Canada.

And so lonely men sit out the eight months of winter at Alert, recording and analyzing these movements. We may never be able to control the weather, but we can now forecast when and where the bad blizzards will strike. Those who pilot the aircraft across the polar lands that lie between the densely populated parts of the world, must know about the weather above these lands, and also about the influence of the northern lights upon their radio equipment. It is to ensure their safe flight that northern scientists probe the atmosphere with rockets and radio waves.

Arctic weather does not stay north of the treeline. Every year cold winds, snow and ice come south. In the arctic, scientists can readily study these processes that make life in the more temperate latitudes difficult, dangerous and expensive during the winter. The potholes that plague the drivers of cars in the south appear to be formed by the same process that causes pingos — ice-cored mounds — to rise above the tundra surface. Studying how pingos are formed may help us to understand how potholes can be prevented.

For more years than we shall ever know, the Eskimo has understood that air is a poor conductor of heat and cold, and he has designed his clothing accordingly. His loose-fitting, air-tight garment allows free movement of the limbs and yet prevents both the escape of body heat and the formation of ice inside his clothing. The caribou, in its coat, utilizes the same secret of insulation against the cold: each hair is a tiny air cell. Following these principles, manufacturers have designed improved winter clothing for all Canadians.

In case the idea of how to dress in cold climates appears obvious, it is worth looking at some of the old prints of British naval men in the arctic. These men wore their heavy sea-going garb, and even cocked hats, when they went ashore; they no doubt considered the Eskimos quaintly dressed. Recent research though has proven the wisdom of the Eskimo-designed clothes.

Fish in the north manage to survive, thrive and reproduce even when lakes and rivers freeze almost to their beds. Ichthyologists and physiologists have studied the processes by which some species adapt to such extreme environments. From their work may come findings that will help man to live and travel in the icy wastes of space.

Ice on rivers, lakes and around the coasts has long presented a problem that has hindered Canadian development. Satellites whirling around the earth can transmit photographs of the ice cover of the arctic, the Gulf of St. Lawrence and subarctic parts of Canada. The extent and movement of this ice can now quickly and accurately be mapped. At Tuktoyaktuk, at the mouth of the Mackenzie River, experiments have been conducted to discover if the arctic coasts can be kept ice-free by bubbling air up from the sea bed through specially installed pipes. The movement of the bubbles circulates the warm water from the bottom, this creates a mixing with the cold water on the top and thus prevents ice from forming. On ships and on glaciers, scientists are studying ice, one of the earth's elemental substances, to determine how Canada's coasts and lands can be made more accessible and habitable, and more than this: in a world facing a shortage of water, Canada possesses a vast resource in the ice which is locked up in the high arctic glaciers and elsewhere.

The north is like a vast outdoor laboratory, where processes can be studied in isolation, and their interaction seen more clearly. Here the caribou live in their "natural" state, moving with the seasons, grazing on the lichens, preyed on by wolves, hunted by man. Here the mosquitoes that make summer life miserable in the bush can be examined as they grow under summer warmth and survive in winter cold. On the margins of existence, plants, animals and men must change and adapt in order to survive the bitter cold.

Canada is a northern nation and the pace of northern development will depend on the sort of questions the scientists in the north ask and the answers they receive. The progress made by the Russians in the arctic has shown how the pace of northern development can be accelerated by knowing and understanding the facts about the north. Development anywhere depends upon discovering the facts about the physical environment and those who inhabit it, and arranging these facts about men and the land into some sort of order. The absence of one small piece of knowledge, as the tragedies of the arctic show, may mean the difference between life and death, between progress and stagnation. Scientists in all fields in all parts of the north are slowly but surely moving towards an understanding of the reality of this strange, empty, appealing land. They are beginning to understand why things and men behave as they do there.

The work of the scientists has no beginning and no end. It is essentially endless, an accumulation of great masses of detail, of painstaking examination of data and careful testing. But the scientist believes that the world is essentially rational and logical. Albert Einstein, the greatest of modern scientists, whose abstract reasoning, complicated equations and constant questioning opened up to mankind the promise and perils of the atomic age, once wrote:

"I cannot believe that God plays dice with the world."

He, like every other scientist, sought order in seeming chaos. He sought the reason for the behaviour of the world inside the atom and beyond the solar system. The northern scientist, whether in an isolated tent or an overheated hut, seeks to unravel the many mysteries of life that can best be studied north of the treeline.

PROF. JIM LOTZ, *Professor and Research Director, Canadian Research Centre for Anthropology, St. Paul University, Ottawa. Born Liverpool, 1929. R.A.F. 1947-49. B.A. (Geography), University of Manchester, 1952. M.Sc. (Geography) McGill University, 1957. Post-graduate work, University of British Columbia, 1964-65. U.S.A.F. Ellesmere Island Ice Shelf Project, 1959. Defence Research Board, 1960. Northern Affairs, Community Planning Officer, 1960-62; Research Officer, Northern Co-ordination and Research Centre. Research on socio-economic development of Yukon Territory (Yukon Research Project), 1962-66.*

PROF. J. J. HONINGMANN

On Understanding
Another People

Although the anthropologist understands the
reason why he might be eaten by a
cannibal this does not necessarily mean
that he agrees with the idea.

Always in dealing with people who live by other customs than we
do, we face the hazard of taking our own customs so much for
granted (as to right and proper) that we judge the ways of other
people only by how close they come to our own. If they don't come
close we call the people primitive, barbarian or sometimes even
worse. But we can never fully understand another society simply by
measuring the extent to which its culture comes up to ours. To
understand another culture (on its own terms) requires that we
temporarily forget our own and adopt a "culturally relative" point
of view.

Cultural relativity means thinking with other rules and standards
than our own while holding our own standards, values and beliefs
in abeyance. This is not always easy, but anthropologists furnish
living proof that with a little practice, cultural relativity can be
mastered. Such mastery offers real advantages. It puts us in a better
position to deal more effectively with other people. It prevents us
from making costly or embarrassing mistakes through misunderstanding other people. It prevents us from distorting other ways of
life by regarding them simply as copies, often inferior copies of our
own, which they never are. Cultural relativity provides us with an
objective basis for understanding people who follow other customs
than we do.

I remember one of my first lessons in cultural relativity some years ago when, together with my wife and children, I was travelling with the Kaska Indians to their winter trapping grounds in southern Yukon Territory. We stopped for lunch, and opened a can of sardines. My wife buttered some bread we had brought along. She made first the children and then me open-faced sandwiches. Old Stuart, a Kaska Indian, watched the preparations with an intentness whose significance I did not grasp until, when my wife handed me the carefully made sandwich, he exploded laughing, "Look, she makes his food for him, as if he were a child." My image of myself suffered at that instant, but I also learned something, my wife and I were not conforming to the Kaska Indian's own standards of proper behaviour. We were acting like Americans.

More recently when I was in Frobisher Bay, I heard teachers, who had come to Baffin Island to teach Eskimo children, complain about Eskimo parents. The teachers claimed that Eskimo parents spoiled the children by allowing them to do whatever they pleased. In a way, the teachers were right, but they distorted what they saw. Compared to the teachers' own standards, Eskimo parents do permit their children considerable emotional spontaneity. The teachers distorted Eskimo parents' behaviour by judging it too much from their own standards of parental discipline. The teachers had little regard for cultural relativity, and as a result they failed to see how consistently Eskimo life encourages children to grow up into independent and very resourceful adult human beings.

Because it takes time and effort to master another culture and to see it in terms of its inherent standards and values, anthropologists make it a point to live in a foreign culture for a long period, humbly learning their hosts' standards and customs. They need plenty of time to get rid of as many prejudices as possible so that they may perceive in a fresh, objective way what the people themselves are doing and why they are doing it.

In the same way that learning a foreign language requires working with the rules of that language, and not the rules of another, learning to understand how Eskimos, Indians or any other people think and act requires that you forget the standards and habits of your own culture and concentrate on the culture you want to understand.

We believe firmly in fighting for our convictions, but it doesn't follow that every society has the same concept of courage. The Samoans studied by Margaret Mead, and described in her famous book *Coming of Age in Samoa*, expect nobody to suffer for the sake of his convictions. Our values and preferences don't fit Samoan culture and we in turn couldn't run our civilization in the way they or the Eskimos run theirs.

Cultural relativity recognizes that behaviour is always appropriate to a particular time and place, to a particular system of culture. Many of our ways of doing things have evolved in our culture through hundreds of years. They can't be fully adopted by other people until those people have sufficiently changed their system, their religion, their ideas, their social relationships, in order that the new forms may fit. Therefore, if people cannot adopt everything we try to teach them, we mustn't jump to the conclusion that they are ignorant or that they are of inferior intelligence. If you use your eyes unbiasedly, you will see that every group of people is intelligent enough to solve their own traditional problems quite efficiently. They have to be, otherwise they wouldn't have survived and wouldn't be here any longer for you to see them; but of course all the individuals of a group won't be equally intelligent. When people do change their way of life, we should understand them sympathetically, in terms of the mistakes we think they are making. Well-meaning people in the north regret to see the Eskimos moving from their camps and settlements into towns like Frobisher Bay and Inuvik. Most of the Eskimos whom I met in Frobisher Bay showed no inclination to return to the small settlements of Baffin Island which they had left. They recalled, without regret, their former hazardous hunting and trapping careers, and much preferred to work in town as drivers, carpenters, cooks or glaziers. They and their families found the jobs, comforts and rich recreational resources of Frobisher Bay town much more satisfactory than their sparse previous culture.

Are there any moral virtues that recur from one culture to another, virtues that we can call truly universal and that moderate cultural relativity? Anthropologists have looked assiduously for universal virtues, and they have found a few. For example, murder of a fellow tribesman is generally condemned in all cultures, and incest with close relatives is practically never tolerated anywhere in the world. Some degree of co-operation is also universally practiced though it may be restricted only to very near relatives. Outweighing such relatively few universal virtues are dozens of discrepant values in which societies diverge. These divergent values make cultural understanding enormously difficult. It is these that call on us to master cultural relativity so that they may be understood.

Cultural relativity doesn't say that everything goes. Anthropologists don't believe that everything is equally good. Some people are cannibals by custom, but no anthropologist would approve of being eaten regardless of how well he understands reasons for the custom.

The world has many governments, each of which operates more or less effectively with its own constitution and laws, but it doesn't follow that all governments are equally good in the moral sense. In other words, cultural relativity isn't at all identical with ethical neutrality or with moral relativity. Headhunting in another culture can be understood without going all out in its support. Successfully to grasp and appreciate standards of beauty, ideas of morality, and rules of correctness in another culture is a most exciting intellectual achievement, but fortunately it doesn't require us to go so far as to say that everything is equally desirable and that nothing is better than anything else.

Anthropologists, in fact, have their own values and opinions that they prefer above others, and that they cling to just as other people cling to theirs. Cultural relativity itself is such a value, one which I have maintained is preferable to being cultural-bound and ethnocentric.

PROF. JOHN J. HONINGMANN, *University of North Carolina. Born New York, 1917. B.A., Brooklyn College, 1942; M.A., Yale, 1943; Ph.D., 1947. Several field trips to interior of British Columbia, Northern Quebec, and Baffin Island.*

ILLUSTRATIONS

52

53

54

55

56

57

58

59

60

61

62

63

N. O. CHRISTENSEN

Greenland

In the realm of cultural relativity and to give an overall picture of life in the arctic, we now take a look at other arctic lands.

Greenland is Canada's second neighbour, your friendly neighbour to the east. To write about Greenland for people in the Canadian north we should deal with the most important part of our country, the people, the Greenlanders, "Kalâtdlit" as they call themselves.

There are today around 36,000 Greenlanders of Eskimo origin. In Greenland, there live also around 3,000 Danes who work there in various kinds of jobs, most of them staying only a few years; a few of them living there most of their lives. Until 1953 Greenland was governed as a colony. By the Danish Constitution of 1953, however, it was accorded the status of a fully integrated part of the kingdom of Denmark, electing two members to the parliament of Denmark. Special Greenland affairs are the responsibility of a cabinet minister for Greenland. Local affairs are handled in part by a popularly elected provincial council, "the Landsraad" and in part by a Danish governor, "the Landshøvding." Despite the fundamental equality between Greenland and the rest of the kingdom, there is a certain amount of special legislation applicable to Greenland.

The Greenlanders take a very active part in the governing of their country. The two present Greenland members to the Danish Parliament, both of them Greenlanders, do not belong to any of the Danish political parties. In the future, however, the Greenland representatives will probably take more and more part in the regular Danish political activities. The 16 elected members of the provincial council have one regular yearly session, usually lasting five to six weeks, and one short extra meeting a year. They are elected by all men and women over the age of 21 years and represent all parts of the island. The Governor is automatically chairman of the council, but a change is expected here in 1967, when the council members will elect their own chairman. The council gets its funds from duty on tobacco, liquor, and the like, adding up yearly to the equivalent of nearly $4,000,000. The council is responsible for the welfare of the Greenlanders and, for example, paying the old-age pension, helping invalids and other social programs. The council also takes an active part in housing programs, building of orphanages, homes for the aged, roads in the settlements. I should also mention that the Greenlanders are responsible for the governing of the local affairs through 16 local municipalities. Space does not allow me to enter into details about these, but I should add that hospitals and schools as well as a loan fund for housing and a loan fund for fishing boats, freezing plants, and stores is government responsibility.

What are our most significant problems at the moment? I think the enormous increase of the population ranks as problem number one. Greenland is among those areas which have the highest increase of population in the world. Almost half — 45 per cent — of all Greenlanders are 15 years of age or younger. We have compulsory schooling for children from seven to 14 years of age. Every year we spend a great deal of money not only for schools, but also on homes for teachers. Today there are 7,000 children in preparatory schools in Greenland. In 1967 there will be 14,000 — this will then include eighth and ninth grades. At the moment many people move from small outposts and camps to the towns, the largest of which is Godthaab with 5,150 inhabitants. All this adds to the problems of schools and housing. Problem number two is of another nature: let us call it the language barrier. The Greenlanders speak an Eskimo tongue. The Danish colonization in Greenland started as early as 1721, but followed for many years (up to the 1950's) a policy of protection: only slowly should the Greenlanders come into contact with western civilization. I am not criticizing this policy, but it is a fact that it has left us with the enormous problem of Greenlanders speaking only the Eskimo language. Only a few of them are able to make themselves understood in Danish, and very few are bilingual.

In most of the schools the children are taught in Eskimo, which in Greenland is a written language. Danish is taught to a great extent, but only effectively in the bigger towns and settlements, and apparently you cannot make a people bilingual that way. The language problem is common for all the Eskimo countries. It is a problem in Alaska, as well as in the Canadian north and Greenland. But in Alaska, it has been the policy of the United States of America to teach in English and only in English. Today nearly all Alaskan Eskimos speak good English. In Canada you have had only a few years of experience, but as the Canadian Eskimos have nearly no literature, your policy will probably have to follow the Alaskan pattern. The Greenlanders love their language; they want to preserve it. On the other hand, they know that their only way to higher education is through Danish. In the outposts, the teachers are Greenlanders and only a few of them are able to teach more than the most basic Danish. In the towns, where two-thirds of the population now live, we have a great number of Danish teachers, but they do not speak Greenlandic. We have only a few fully bilingual teachers. The result of all this is that only a limited number of young Greenlanders enter high school, where only Danish is spoken — even if they have the brains, they can't always jump the language barrier. A proposal for a new school law has recently been placed before the provincial council; if this passes the legislature, we will get better means of teaching more children Danish, but we still have a long way to go to make an appreciable number of Greenlanders really bilingual.

Such are the two major problems — the increase in population, and the language barrier. Space does not allow me to enter deeper into the many other difficulties we are up against. Some of them, by the way, are very familiar to you in the Canadian north.

During the past years much has been done to improve the conditions in Greenland economically, socially and culturally. Every year millions are invested in development. In the process a great number of Danish skilled labour and management people are brought in. These people do not speak or understand any Greenlandic. Here you also have the language barrier. Many Greenlanders feel that they are just sitting by the roadside looking at all that happens in their country. They do not feel that they participate. The psychological effect is not very good. In certain cases, it forms political problems of the most unfortunate nature.

To look at the economy of Greenland, the three main enterprises are first, seal-hunting, carried on mainly in the northern part of the west coast and on the east coast, secondly, fishing, which is important for the rest of the country, and finally sheep farming, that gives a limited number of farmers a good living in the farthest south. The future of Greenland lies in the great fishing banks off southern Greenland, with some of the richest codfish banks in the world. Great foreign fishing fleets now harvest these banks nearly all year round. The Greenlanders' fishing up till now has been mainly limited to the coastal waters and the fiords, as they do not have big fishing vessels and trawlers that can fish all year round in the open sea. Moreover, very few Greenlanders have the education to man such ships, except in the lowest positions. Greenlandic fishermen only take around 10 per cent of the fish that is caught along the Greenland coast. Other nations take the rest. A program of education in navigation and fishing techniques is now being launched, and in the coming year money will be invested in bigger fishing vessels, and in the fishing industries. Many people from outposts and less prosperous areas of the country are expected to move to towns where they can make a living as fishermen or factory workers. Their children would receive better schooling than in the remote areas.

It will take years, many years, but we are optimistic here in Greenland, and we have reason to be so. Since the war ended, the economy of the Greenlanders has improved considerably. Many hundreds of new homes have been built, hundreds of new classrooms have been opened, but our share of the riches of our seas is only 10 per cent. When the Greenlandic fishermen can manage the modern fishing equipment, when freezing plants are built in all the towns and the Greenlanders have the technical skill to run these themselves, when thousands of new homes have been built to allow the population to concentrate in a few rather big cities, we shall see not the end, but the end of the beginning.

N. O. CHRISTENSEN, *Governor of Greenland. Born Denmark, 1917. Law degree, University of Copenhagen. Entered Greenland Service, 1945. Appointed District Commissioner in Northern Greenland, 1947. Deputy to the Governor of Greenland, 1950-56. Greenland Department in Denmark, 1956-62. Appointed Governor of Greenland, 1962 until the present time.*

DR. TERENCE ARMSTRONG

Russia

*How far have achievements in the Soviet arctic
outpaced those in Canada's north?
Nobody seems to know for sure; what follows
are the educated guesses of a man who is
probably the most knowledgeable in the west
about matters Soviet.*

The Soviet slice of the arctic is much the biggest slice. The Arctic
Circle runs through Soviet territory for nearly half its total length,
Canadian territory for under a quarter — 164° and 80° respectively.
So there is roughly twice as much Soviet northland as Canadian
northland.

But perhaps even more important than the size is the length of
time the Russians have been up in the north doing things. For at
least 800 years they have been familiar with the European north,
the White Sea region especially, and for over 300 years they have
known the rest of it right through to Bering Strait. Their advance
from the Urals to the Pacific took only 60 years to cover a distance
of 3,000 miles. The driving force behind it all was the search for
fur, a commodity much more widely used then than now, and once
the fur traders and the Cossacks got into the north, they stayed
there. For many generations the Russians have known how to live
and work in the north. This is certainly one of the important facts
which helps one understand their present performance there.
Another is that much more recently, in the early years of the Soviet
regime, the country was weak and isolated and it was quite clear
that if she was going to become strong, the resources for this must
be found on her own territory. So the search was started and sure
enough all sorts of mineral riches were found, often in remote parts
of the north; and while other countries might prefer, because it
was cheaper, to buy from friendly neighbours, the Soviet govern-

ment was going it alone and had to find a way of developing these northern resources.

The way it found the solution was to spend much money on exploration and research, on building up a transport network, on training cadres. It was also ruthless, staggeringly ruthless, in its search for less skilled manpower. For it is clear now that much of what was started in the 'thirties and 'forties could not have got going at all without the forced labour of hundreds of thousands of men. Once going, however, it is not so difficult to keep it going. The forced labour system has greatly diminished in the last 10 years, but the undertakings it started up are still flourishing. Evidently other methods are now used to attract workers. The main one at present seems to be the well-tried capitalist one of offering incentives graded to the remoteness of the area. Some of these are in privileges rather than in cash, but a man can be anywhere between two and three and a half times better off if he elects to work in the north, and signs on for several years. It is clear that there are at the moment somewhere between three and four million Russians living in that part of the Soviet Union which roughly corresponds to the Northwest Territories and the Yukon Territory. Besides these immigrants, there are about a million natives up there too: Komi, Yakut, Chukchi, Eskimo and a dozen other peoples. With all of these human beings around it is possible, even if the territory is vast, to make quite a dent in the resources.

This, of course, is what is now being done. The predominant activity is mining. Even before the Revolution, there had been important gold mines in the north. Now there are many more — gold being the chief source of foreign currency — and to them have been added nickel mines, tin mines, diamond mines, coal mines and most recently an immense oil and gas field, in the West Siberian plain, just beginning to produce. All of these have national rather than local significance, and the northern gold, nickel, tin and diamonds are mainstays of the country's production of these minerals. Output figures are not published, presumably for strategic reasons, but the nickel mining town of Noril'sk near the mouth of the Yenisey River has reached a population of over 120,000 in its 30 years of existence. So the scale of this operation is clearly big. In the last couple of years a very extensive new ore body has been found a few miles away, so this is to be no boom and bust town.

The Canadian north has a big mining potential too, but there is no development yet on anything like the same scale as Noril'sk. Yellowknife, Keno Hill and other places are important in the Canadian economy, but they mostly employ a few hundred people as against tens of thousands. Nor is the Canadian potential as fully explored as the Soviet. In short, Canada has not yet gone so far as the Soviet Union in this whole question of northern minerals.

It is a tremendous job, obviously, to keep settlements of this size re-supplied, and there are eight towns of over 50,000 in the Soviet arctic and subarctic. A big effort is made to produce food locally. Fisheries probably contribute the most. The big Siberian rivers are rich in fish, and under-ice fishing techniques make year-round catches possible. They have a flourishing reindeer industry, with two million domesticated reindeer in the country, and they probably yield enough meat for nearly 200,000 people. Specialized farms, some with glasshouses, produce vegetables and milk, but they can't go more than a small distance towards meeting the demand. But taken together, all these local food sources must help significantly to reduce the large freighting bill on bringing in supplies from the south. It is in this sector that the northern peoples make the greatest contribution. They have been fishing, and herding reindeer for centuries, and their skill at these is utilized rather than ignored, as would be the case if they were put down in the mines.

The transport system has become pretty effective too, since without it, none of the productive activity could go on. Waterways are the highways, as they have been in Canada, and there are well-equipped river fleets connecting upstream to railhead and downstream to the Northern Sea Route, the old Northeast Passage. There's also an efficient air network. On land, however, again as in Canada, there is very little.

The Soviet north, then, seems to be very much a going concern, but there are two things to be mentioned here. First, almost all of the information I have quoted comes out of books, Soviet books. Very few qualified observers from the outside have checked it on the ground. Mr. Arnold Smith, recently Canadian Ambassador in Moscow, and Mr. Arthur Laing during his tenure as Minister of Northern Affairs, in the Canadian government, are two of these very few, and only a corner of the curtain was lifted for them. But even so, it is most unlikely that the Soviet story is all propaganda.

Second, no one outside the Soviet Union, and perhaps no one inside it either, can say whether it all pays in the sense we understand that term. Under private enterprise, I am pretty sure a good deal of this activity would not have got going at all. But one of the advantages of the Soviet system is that undertakings like these, whose immediate future in terms of profit and loss is hard to predict, can be got underway, if there are other factors in their favour, more easily than under our system.

And that is a relevant point when one comes to consider what Canada can learn from the Soviet Union in this field. The way they operate, the decision-reaching process is so different from the western way that there is not too much helpful comparison to be made. But at the level of techniques, of methods and design, there are lots and lots of notes to be compared and this I am glad to say, is being done more and more. Each country is trying to subdue the same sort of environment, and the answers each gets are bound to be interesting to the other. What about those Soviet reindeer, for instance? A herd that size could feed the whole population of the Canadian north and still leave plenty for sale outside. The Soviet Union, it must be admitted, has the easier time of it. Nature has endowed her north more bountifully, with more fertile soil, a much more convenient river system, and warmer summers, leading to a more northerly treeline. She may have twice the area of the Canadian northland, but she has also got ten times Canada's population, so a much higher level of development is to be expected. Canada is pulling up fast, however, and already the Soviet Union is showing signs of keen interest in Canadian achievements. Canada has much to gain by making this link as strong as possible.

DR. TERENCE ARMSTRONG, *Assistant Director of Research, Scott Polar Institute, Cambridge University. Born Surrey, England, 1920. Read modern languages including Russian at Cambridge. Ph.D., Cambridge, 1951. Honorary law degree, McGill, during International Arctic Symposium, 1963. Extensive travel in Scandinavian countries and three trips to the U.S.S.R. On board HMS Labrador through Northwest Passage, 1954. Member Royal Central Asian Society, Glaciological Society, and American Association for the Advancement of Slavic Studies. Fellow of Royal Geographical Society and Arctic Institute of North America.*

84

DR. WILLIAM IRVING

Alaska

In 1867 it was sold for 2 cents per acre, or
1/22,000 of a cent per square foot.
Would it be possible to put a monetary
value on it today?

Alaska has been since 1959 one of the 50 American states, with
the same political and economic institutions as the others. Its population is largely of white American origin, drawn mainly from the
western states but with a sizable increment coming from the south
and the east. At the same time many things tend to make the state
unique: its large size, some 586,000 square miles, its geographical
isolation from the rest of the United States and, indeed, from any
centre of population, and the small number of its inhabitants — not
yet 300,000 — come most readily to mind. Alaska's closest neighbours, the Yukon Territory and northern British Columbia, share
with it a history of gold rushes, mining development and fur trade.
The Yukon and adjacent Alaska were only nominally distinguished
until the boundary survey of 1911, and there still are many
Yukoners who lived for a time in Alaska. The state shares with
Florida and Nevada the highest rate of population increase in the
United States — over 75 per cent between 1950 and 1960. More
than 100,000 motor vehicles ply its long highways, a rather large
number when you consider that probably a quarter of the people
live in towns and villages without any road connection with the
state highway system. Just as in other parts of the north, air
transport plays a vital role in commerce and administration, to say
nothing of science and social relations. Scheduled air lines, "air
taxi" operators, and private light planes compete in flight patterns
with military and other government aircraft, so that the congestion
in air lanes around the cities of Anchorage and Fairbanks is a
matter of concern.

Less than 40 per cent of Alaskans live in the seven communities classed as urban, with more than 2,500 inhabitants, and the great majority of these live in Anchorage or Fairbanks, which also have large suburban developments around them. It is fair to say that, except for geographical peculiarities, these two principal cities, and Juneau, the capital, are much like any of comparable size in the more recently settled parts of northwestern states. Paved streets frequently under repair, high-rise apartments, and supermarkets, if they be marks of progress, place these communities in the forefront of advancing civilization. Most of their inhabitants, native Alaskans and whites alike, are employed in transportation, retail or whole-sale trade, one of the service trades, or professional or administrative positions in government, construction or mining. The proportion of skilled to unskilled labor appears to be very high. The cost of living, too, is very high, but so is the annual income *per capita* which throughout the state averages well over $3,000 and among city dwellers may be half again as much.

A glance at any of the recently published histories of Alaska will show that, whereas high prices have always prevailed, statehood, cities, and a system of transport remarkably efficient by northern standards have all come about since the end of World War II. Although economic booms and busts have been characteristic of the Alaskan economy since the 18th century, and a prehistorian may guess since long before that, this boom is unprecedented in magnitude and in its effect on the population and on the country-side. Its causes are, of course, complex. Common belief rates as important the initiative of military personnel and construction men who came to the territory during and shortly after the war. Improve-ments in the technology and regulation of transport in post-war years, and an unsettled international situation, motivated the American federal government at that time to spend a great deal of money to establish air bases and their supporting establishments, which in turn encouraged men in the private search for wealth, and companies in the discovery and development of new resources. Although federal government spending is still the most important element in the Alaskan economy, private industry with "outside" capital now is playing a larger role than it did before and there is reasonable hope for continuing prosperity, and even stability inde-pendent of massive government support. At the same time, a great effort is being made to ensure that the economy of the state develops in ways favourable to Alaskan residents, with diversified industry supported in part by local investment. As evidence of the confidence of Alaskans in their own economy, consider the impressive support now given the expanding state university and its affiliated institutes, and the speed and thoroughness of Anchorage's recovery from the effects of the Good Friday earthquake of 1964.

But if the cities and industry afford one aspect of Alaska, the outlying towns and villages give another, and one not so easy to sum up. And one cannot ignore either the large number of scientific and exploratory enterprises, which in one sense link villages with the cities and the world "outside," but which in a sense more important to the world at large, contribute much to the vitality of both the state and of their several disciplines.

The villages, though small and scattered, are important as sources of manpower, as bases for exploration, and as reservoirs of native culture. One reason for differences among them is the diversity of the environments they occupy, which range from north temperate to arctic, and from maritime to mountain. Another is the number of native cultures, which really can't be counted, and the varying degree of acculturation, which can't be measured. There are eight major languages spoken in addition to English, and each of the eight comprises several subsidiary tongues mutually intelligible only with difficulty, if at all. Furthermore, the villages, in addition to being strongly affected by their local environments are, many of them, unlike the cities, strongly rooted in their own history which in some cases goes back a thousand years or more. Some are incredibly poor and seem doomed to extinction without a new outside source of revenue. Others, almost wholly dependent on subsistence hunting and fishing, or on single industries such as a fish cannery or a gold mine, have an uncertain future. Still others have recently become important transport depots and will certainly continue to grow. Some farming communities, almost entirely white American, appear well established and viable, especially those in the Matunuska Valley, but there are new ones near Fairbanks as well, that show promise.

One of the most significant things about Alaska's small communities, for an "outsider," is that they are undergoing rapid cultural evolution isolated from one another, except for links provided by Euro-American culture. The United States, and Alaska in particular, will benefit from this process, which already has produced outstanding men known for their contributions to commerce, journalism, and science. The biological principal of hybrid vigor seems here to have a very close cultural analogue. The fact that men whose grandparents lived in the Stone Age are now commercial airline pilots and concert pianists suggests that there are other things as well to be learned from Alaska's Indians and Eskimos.

If some Alaskan natives are remarkably adept in modern American ways by comparison with aborigines in other places, why is this so? To twist a phrase, their native abilities are of course high; their other native endowments are also important though incalculable. But Indians in South Dakota and New Mexico, for example, where there are large Indian populations, don't hold office in state legislatures as do some Alaskan natives, although they have produced distinguished men in the past. Something has given a few Alaskan natives a running head start into American culture of the 1960's; as a prehistorian I feel that I must look to the past for an explanation. One factor is that no Alaskan natives have been chased from hunting grounds by ranchers or farmers. A few may have been displaced by urban sprawl, but most have moved toward what appeared, rightly or wrongly, to be greater opportunity. They have retained the habit of seeking the best way to make a living and to get on in society. Another factor is the example of white men who have frequented or lived in native villages since the late 19th century. Their example, in what passed for technology and business administration on the frontier, was cogent and appropriate because most of them were committed to self-interest rather than to the interest of a government, a church, or a corporation. They were poor men bent on getting rich; not quite like the Peace Corps, but they were and are similar if you disregard motive and some aspects of conduct, for a good number of them lived in the villages rather than adjacent to them. Without such a resident group of exemplars, it is doubtful that Alaskan natives could have adapted to the new conditions as well as they have.

But those notably successful Indians and Eskimos of whom I speak made their entry into urban-industrial culture several decades ago. How well prepared are the younger Alaskan natives for life in an American state? Although most have gone to schools taught in English, many have trouble with such things as a mail order catalogue. Too many still enter our society at its lowest level, where ignorance is not a handicap but wisdom is not an asset. And times are changing. Whereas once the ingenious, self-reliant pioneer could teach a native Alaskan nearly all he needed to know about the new society, now only formal education and the new example of the organization man will suffice. Of course, this situation is not peculiar to Alaska or to the north. But it places a particularly heavy burden of responsibility on the new state school system, which is taking over the federal government schools for natives and is charged with the education of all who meet academic requirements through university to graduate degrees.

As an amusing and instructive example of two cultures making common cause against an outside threat, consider the recent plight of some white men employed by a government contractor in an Eskimo village, the contractor, ostensibly to protect the Eskimo, but, we may reasonably suspect, more in order to suppress liaisons and embarrassing *sequelae*, imposed a curfew at night on the white members of its mixed white and Eskimo crew. But when the curfew was enforced, it developed that a number of the white men were married to Eskimo women in the village. The contractor maintained the curfew with threats of dismissal against all who violated it, until the matter came to the attention of the *Tundra Times,* a newspaper run by and for Alaskan natives. With characteristic zeal the *Times* laid the case before the public, and the affected families were quickly reunited. We are not told by the *Times,* from which this story comes, whether this incident had any overall effect on the personnel policies of the contractor.

DR. WILLIAM IRVING, *National Museum of Canada. Born Toronto, 1927. B.A., Anthropology, University of Alaska, 1952; attended Harvard, 1953-57; Ph.D., University of Wisconsin, 1965. Field work in Alaska, United States and Mexico; Archaeological and Ethnological reconnaissance in District of Keewatin, 1960, 1963, 1964. Research Assistant in Anthropology, University of Wisconsin. Fellow Arctic Institute of North America and of the American Association for the Advancement of Science.*

DR. GEERT VAN DEN STEENHOVEN

The Law Through Eskimo Eyes

A good hunter and meat provider in an Eskimo community is a man of stature and, because of this, he is allowed a certain margin when it comes to moral behaviour.

It is by now common knowledge that the Eskimos — I am thinking chiefly of those living in the Keewatin District — have no tradition of political entities like tribes, with their councils, and common meetings and rituals. Only two social entities play a role of importance in their daily existence: their circle of relatives, and the camp to which they belong at a given moment. The family circle has approximately the same composition as what we westerners call "our family." The mutual affection between these kinfolk is quite considerable and social intercourse, economic co-operation, marriage arrangements and adoption take place preferably within this circle.

Authority within the family rests with the husband of the elementary family — i.e., father, mother and children. Beyond the elementary family, authority rests with the oldest brother over both his own elementary family and those of his younger brothers and of his sons. And that is all the recognized and — however informally — institutionalized authority there exists. Among these nomadic people, the camp, that important community of daily life and work, has as such no leader, though one of the heads of its constituent families may incidentally enjoy enough prestige to see at times his important decisions voluntarily followed by non-related camp fellows. As a rule, camps have a fluctuating population of five to ten (rarely more) elementary families, several of which are usually related to each other. Each family, or set of families under one family head, is fully autonomous. Common residence in a camp creates certain rights and duties with regard to camp members, even if they are not related. In short, there exists a certain recognized authority within elementary and extended families — but beyond this there is no common institutionalized leadership, not even in the camp.

The question arises as to how social control or social order is ensured within this small and isolated camp community. How did these traditionally leaderless communities manage to survive when the peace of the camp, in its medieval sense of the regular, ordered course of affairs, was felt to be threatened? In order to find the answer, we must realize that it does not involve the idea of justice. This is a highly abstract concept which the Eskimos do not think about, nor is the idea of punishment their primary aim. We should rather think of their aim in terms of getting rid of someone who is felt by the camp to have become a nuisance, whether he can help it or not.

What kind of behaviour is likely to make people a nuisance to their camp fellows? The cases which I recorded seem to show that the community does not feel itself threatened so much by the mere fact that someone killed someone else, if only he was known as a generally good and trustworthy camp member and hunter. People are likely to disapprove of murder as such, but as long as they understand the murderer's motivation, and as long as repetition on his part was not anticipated, the community *per se* did not seem to be much involved. Indeed, the peace of the camp appears to be upset by the man who shows himself to be unreliable, a liar, a man whose conduct is unpredictable, and who may cause daily annoyance and inconvenience.

There are the lazy hunters, and the families who without good reason fail to adhere to the food-sharing customs, and the undesirable, i.e., non-conforming, newcomers. It would therefore seem that the Eskimo community, in trouble cases affecting only some of its members or the camp itself, judges the contestant or the wrongdoer not so much on the ground of his objective act, but rather in the light of his total social position in the camp. This is where other considerations come in, such as his efficiency as a hunter, his song-composing qualities, his shamanistic healing powers, in short, his general sociability and usefulness as a camp member. Among these qualities, the importance of being a good hunter and provider of meat for the camp is prominent. I recall the story of a man, still living among the Netsilingmiut who 50 years ago murdered a camp fellow in order to marry his wife. He fled north with her, but in due time returned to his people where he raised a respected family. I found that the Eskimos of his community still disapprove of the murder. Why? Not because of the Ten Commandments, in spite of their baptism of 25 years ago and their sincere devotion to the Christian faith, but "because the man who was killed was a much better hunter and meat provider than the man who killed him."

If the community feels one of its members is an undesirable element and a really bad nuisance, it will tend to rid itself of him, and that in characteristically Eskimo manner, either by indirectly forcing him to leave, or by social withdrawal from him, or, but this only in the case of a dangerous sorcerer or insane person, by consenting to the decision of his family members to let him be "executed" by his nearest relative. The Eskimo way of social withdrawal from a nuisance, which I found most strongly among the Caribou Eskimos, is a gradual and spontaneous process in which such a man no longer receives visits from the others, no longer shares in their hunting plans, and finally finds himself suddenly deserted because the rest of the camp has moved elsewhere in his absence. Often, the social reaction will go on further than a certain degree of social withdrawal. Although this never implies that one would not hand a bit of food to such an undesirable neighbour if, even through his fault, he, his wife and children were hungry, such a man will as a rule find it an unbearable thing to stand alone against all others. The Eskimo way of "forcing one to leave" is applied with their sharpest weapon: continuous ridiculing and making fun of someone to the point of forcing him to conform or to leave. Again, the community is both party to and judge of a process which gradually and spontaneously develops without any formalities whatsoever. This ridiculing habit I found most pronouncedly enforced among the Netsilingmiut.

The well-known song-duel between individual contestants has some institutionalized features, though much less developed in

Canada than in Greenland. Both adversaries try to ridicule each other in the eyes of all bystanding camp fellows by singing satirical ballads at each other while dancing with the drum, until the onlookers by their increasing handclapping indicate the "winner," upon which the loser often, out of shame, leaves the camp temporarily or permanently.

In most conflicts between individuals, however, the community as such does not intervene, leaving the conflicting parties to themselves or their families. The absence of social patterns for the solution or settlement of disputes and tensions may then lead to an "avoiding of each other" or to violence. For when an Eskimo saw no way out from an obsessing problem, then at a given moment the killing of his opponent or "stand-in-his-way" seemed to him the only solution. In the Netsilik area, I noticed that the desire to have a certain married woman as one's wife regularly led to the murdering of her husband, often upon the instigation of the woman herself. Upon such a killing, blood-revenge might follow, either at once or in the course of time, and this could create a long-term climate of general suspicion in which one started to fear almost everyone else. In such situations, new violence purely out of fear might follow. Indeed, these private vengeances and family feuds among persons or groups from different camps must at times have seriously upset the communities involved. It is my impression that the Eskimo camp, in the absence of any inter-community super-structure, was unable to apply a brake to such violence and threat of violence, except by persuading the family of a victim not to take revenge — as indeed appears not seldom to have been the case. Another feud-preventing circumstance could occur when some people were members both of the group seeking revenge and of the group against which the revenge is apt to be directed.

Everyone who has observed Eskimos in Keewatin, will agree that their social existence in small groups does not call for fixed rules or structured rulership. Instead, all aspects of their social life are characterized by an admirable flexibility enabling them, under hard physical conditions, not only to survive but even to produce works of art, especially in their oral literature and poetry. In the years of my visits to the Keewatin District, these small communities were carrying on admirably. Violence had now practically ceased among them. Though justice as an independent concept was not known among them, there was a strong feeling for fair and reasonable practices in routine daily interactions. They certainly have definite opinions on right or wrong, on mine and thine, but these are governed by common sense, realism, self-criticism and a happy absence of righteousness.

Fortunately, trouble was no favoured pastime for these people. One of the most respected and courageous Caribou Eskimos once declared to me, "In cases of dispute and trouble, I would rather run away than fight." And a young hunter from the same region, whom I asked the, admittedly rather silly and abstract, question of what he would do if they had to put up with a trouble-making camp member, answered, "We won't care for him, but we won't let him starve." Then, as if to correct himself, and perhaps remembering his experiences with white men, he added, "An *Eskimo,* however, would always be likeable!"

DR. GEERT VAN DEN STEENHOVEN, *Lecturer in Eskimo Ethnography and customary law of non-western societies at the Catholic University, Nijmegen, The Netherlands. Law degree, University of Leiden; M.A. in Anthropology, University of Toronto, 1953. Sailor on board Regina Polaris on her last arctic season, 1951. Field work Eskimo Point and Ennadai Lake, 1955, and around Pelly Bay 1957.*

MARK M. DE WEERDT

The Law Through Our Eyes

Present day laws even in our newly
developed areas are a living thing with roots
way back in the past.

The Yukon and the Northwest Territories make up about one-half of the land area of Canada. Yet the total population of that half is only about 40,000 divided into three, roughly equal groups, Indians, Eskimos and others. Canada acquired the area which makes up the Territories in 1870 and 1880. The mainland came to us in 1870 together with what is now Alberta, Saskatchewan and Manitoba, while the Arctic Islands came to us 10 years later. The Parliament of Great Britain, which had constituted Canada as a dominion under the British North America Act of 1867, passed in 1905 further acts creating the three prairie provinces out of the old Northwest Territories. Britain at the same time imposed a solemn obligation on Canada to provide peace and order, as well as good government. After 1905 Canada was left with the responsibility and the power to govern what was left of the old Territories, after the three prairie provinces had been carved out. This is the area which now comprises the Yukon and Northwest Territories.

To meet the gold rush in the Klondike, Canada sliced off the region which is now known as the Yukon and passed a special act for its government as a separate territory. Although the gold rush crisis ended long ago, this division of the north into two territories has remained, so that the north is now governed under two separate sets of territorial laws and administrations, both of which to some extent are supervised and controlled from Ottawa. As the northern territories had been acquired from Britain, the English law applied to them at the time of their acquisition by Canada. To this day, in all matters which have not otherwise been provided for by statute the law of England as of 1870 continues to apply in the territories. The same sort of situation exists in all of the provinces except Quebec, which derives its civil law from France rather than England. To speak of present day law in Canada, is to speak not only of law that was laid down this year, 10 years ago or even a 100 years ago. It is to speak of something that has roots in time long before history was written, and has slowly evolved over many centuries with the pace of change increasing in recent years; in the north during the last 25 years especially.

Our law, in other words, consists of much more than black letters on the page of a book. The black letters must be understood in their context, and this context is nothing less than our whole tradition from the early dawn of time down to the present day. As our territorial constitution develops, we keep coming up against situations very similar to those which arose from time to time in the past, as the constitutional models upon which we base our system of parliamentary democracy in Canada were themselves developing, through earlier stages. The territorial constitution is also of great importance because it provides us with a bridge between the fairly sophisticated legal ideas which we use today and earlier ideas which are still held by so-called "primitive peoples." Our legal heritage is able to put us in touch with those earlier ideas, and to help us find ways of adapting new laws to fit ancient situations which are still with us. The criticisms, which are sometimes heard with reference to the application of present-day law to Indians and Eskimos in the north, are for this reason not always fair or well-informed. It is true that there is grave danger of passing inappropriate or oppressive laws when those to whom the laws are applied have no voice in the process which molds the laws. An important step towards removal of this danger was taken when federal franchise was granted to the inhabitants of the eastern arctic in 1962. It is now generally hoped that the people of the eastern arctic soon will also be able to vote in territorial elections.[1]

Much is being done in the schools to put the younger generation of Indians and Eskimos in possession of a sufficient understanding of our way of doing things, to permit them to participate as fully as possible in the processes of democratic self-government. But even if Indian and Eskimo people are, at the present time, able to enter

[1]Ed. note: The first elections in the eastern arctic were held during September, 1966.

fully into these processes, much would still depend on the administrators, charged with responsibility for giving practical effect to these laws, and much would still depend on the law courts. The law courts stand as a sort of touch-stone of the law from day to day, and from year to year. It is often through the courts that the law has grown and has been changed to meet new situations and challenges. And it is through the courts, presided over by men thoroughly steeped in history and tradition of our system of government and law, that due allowance can be made for the circumstances of each case as it arises. Thus the courts can from time to time check the application of new law, and prevent it from becoming oppressive or unrealistic. Thus, they can, if the need arises, call attention to old laws which are still a useful part of the working legal fabric. If the Territorial Council has left a gap, which will require the enactment of new law, or if some existing law has had unjust results, the court can point out the situation if no other remedy exists.

For an example, take the Eskimo marriage case decided a few years ago by the Territorial Court of the Northwest Territories. In that case, a young widow claimed for herself and her infant child an estate of over $25,000. There was no record of the marriage because she and her late husband had not taken out a license, having been married in accordance with Eskimo custom in a remote region on the east coast of Baffin Island. Both were Eskimos. The Marriage Ordinance did not say that such a marriage would be without legal effect, although it did say that a license should be taken out whenever a marriage is solemnized. The question, therefore, arose as to whether the claimants to the estate were, by law, the lawful widow and child of the deceased. The Territorial Court having heard evidence and legal argument in the case, found that the marriage was valid under the law of England of 1870, and in accordance with established Eskimo custom going back to time immemorial. Since there was nothing in the Marriage Ordinance to say that the marriage should not have legal status, it was held that the failure to take out a license did not render the marriage invalid.

And so this custom received legal protection as part of present-day law in the Northwest Territories. Had the court found otherwise, many other Eskimo marriages would have been called into question, and the legitimacy of a large number of Eskimo children would have been rendered, at best, very doubtful. Yet, that was the interpretation of the law which certain administrators would have applied to the case if it had not been for the far deeper knowledge of the law, and the greater insight, which was shown by the Territorial Court.

That was a comparatively simple and straightforward case. Not all of them are as clear-cut as that, and until there is full participation by the Indian and Eskimo people in the affairs of the two territorial governments, it is unlikely that more appropriate laws can be passed. Cases of this kind are likely to arise for some time. Sometimes, as in the Eskimo marriage case, the courts will show how the existing law is sufficient to meet a situation. In other cases, as in the famous duck case, the courts were in the end obliged to find that the Migratory Birds Convention Act applied to Indians as to the rest of us, thus prohibiting them from hunting ducks during the closed season. The courts can point out where the law ought to be changed, and then it is up to the legislature to decide if a change should be made. Either way, problems in the application of our laws will continue to arise with reference to the Eskimo and Indian population as well as in other respects.

The important thing is that these problems can be aired, examined and recorded, and that solutions for them can be found where there is a need. To neglect or refuse to apply the law to the Indian and Eskimo populations is not the answer. Arbitrary administrative choice or capricious discretion would be no better than creating a special status and special law for them which would, in the end, do a great deal more harm than good because then we would be separating them from the rest of us.

However, the law, as it stands, has within itself a great adaptability to widely varied circumstances. This will do much to make its application to the challenging conditions of the north a matter of practical day-to-day reality, so that as the north changes the law will keep pace with that change.

MARK M. DE WEERDT, *Barrister and Solicitor, Yellowknife. Born Cologne, West Germany, 1928. M.A. (Glasgow) 1949. R.C.M.P. 1950-52. Bachelor of Laws (British Columbia) 1955. Called to the Bar of British Columbia, 1956. Practised law with the City Solicitor for Victoria; served as an Advisory Counsel, Justice Department, Ottawa, until 1958. Private practice since at Yellowknife. Travelled widely throughout the North as Crown Attorney for the Northwest Territories. President of N.W.T. Bar Association, Trustee, Yellowknife Public School Board, and various other positions held.*

DR. RICHARD SLOBODIN

Indian Living ... Old Style

*To the early Europeans who came in contact
with the Canadian Indians some
of their customs might have appeared
rather bizarre, but in the
Indian society they were necessary.*

Most of us who live outside of the north think of American Indians as the people who used to hunt buffalo on the plains, carve totem poles on the Pacific Coast, or raise corn, hunt deer, and paddle birch-bark canoes in the eastern forests. We are likely to think of Indians as temperate-zone people and, although we know there are many in the northern parts of the provinces, the far north is not associated with Indians in popular thought, but rather, with Eskimos. As a matter of fact, in the Canadian and Alaskan subarctic, there lived, at the time the Europeans arrived, some 80,000 to 90,000 Indians. Almost half of their homeland was, and is, north of Eskimo territory. It happens that in Canada, the arctic extends in the east far south of the subarctic in the west; that is why many Indians live north of Eskimos.

"Eskimos are a people distinct in physical appearance, in language, and in customs from all the Indian tribes of America." These are the words of Dr. Diamond Jenness, Canada's leading authority on our aboriginal peoples. In physical type, Eskimos are much more closely related to the ancient Mongoloid stock of eastern Asia than the Indians. The Eskimo household is for the most part coastal, and Eskimos make their living largely from the sea. Indians of the north are inland people. Both these facts suggest that the ancestors of the Eskimos migrated to America from Asia later than the various ancestors of the Indians, a supposition which is bolstered by archaeological and other kinds of evidence.

Besides the coastal versus inland distinction between Eskimo and Indian territory, the other chief difference is that the northern Indians dwell in the subarctic life-zone, although some of them are above the Arctic Circle, whereas Canadian Eskimos live in the true arctic life-zone. Winter in the subarctic is just as cold and almost as long as in the arctic, but subarctic summers are warm, permitting the growth of much vegetation, including forests. Summer in the true arctic is cool; the soil hardly thaws at all, and there is no tree cover.

The 80,000 to 90,000 subarctic Indians occupied an area in Canada and Alaska about as large as all of Canada. If one considers that Canada, with 20 million inhabitants, is a sparsely-populated nation, it is evident that the subarctic Indians were thinly scattered indeed. They lived, throughout much of the year, in family groupings. Only occasionally were there gatherings for ceremonials, or for large-scale hunting and fishing. The people who gathered together belonged to related families, spoke the same dialect, and considered themselves to be of one local group — a band, we may call it.

There are a number of languages spoken by the northern Indians, but all are classed by linguistic scholars into two great language families: Algonkian in the east, and Athapaskan in the west. The Algonkian languages of the subarctic include Malecite, Naskapi, Montagnais, Ojibwa, and Cree. The subarctic Athapaskan languages include Chipewyan, Beaver, Sekani, Slavey, Tutchone, and many others.

As has been mentioned, the societies of the northern Indians were not very complicated. Generally speaking, these societies and the ways of life of the people, become somewhat more complex as one goes from east to west across the northern part of the continent. Roughly intermediate are the Kutchin, who speak an Athapaskan language and live on both sides of the Arctic Circle in extreme northwestern Canada and eastern Alaska. Their homeland, neighbouring that of the Eskimos, extends north to the limit of trees, which is here within 50 miles of the Arctic Ocean. The eastern or Canadian Kutchin are commonly known as the Loucheux.

An advantage in focusing upon the Kutchin is that they have not been involved in the fur trade for nearly as long as have more southerly subarctic peoples such as the Cree and the Chipewyan, nor have they been greatly influenced by the wealthy "totem-pole" tribes of the Pacific Coast, as have the Tutchone, Sekani, and Carrier.

When Europeans first encountered them, the Kutchin probably comprised nine bands, of which four lived in what is now Canadian territory. Each band had a territory within which it hunted and fished to make its living. Their country, covered with spruce forest, was rich in game. Woodland caribou were not to be found in millions, as were the barren ground caribou east of the Mackenzie River, but they were plentiful enough. In addition there were moose, sheep, a rich variety of migratory wildfowl, and for the humbler, everyday catch, the snowshoe rabbit and many kinds of freshwater fish.

When migrating caribou were located, the people camped and hunted in a large group, perhaps 200 people, a majority of the band. Caribou were sometimes stampeded over cliffs, but the favourite method of getting them on a large scale was by means of a surround or stockade of stout fencing that might be a mile or more in diameter. Toward the opening in the surround converged two lines of posts extending for several miles. The best young runners were sent out to drive the caribou along the funnel of posts and into the surround, where many were shot with bow and arrow. Construction of the surround and funnel approach, and the conduct of the hunt, give evidence of the organization of co-operative labour on a fairly large scale.

Under certain conditions, for instance when caribou were scattered or absent, the people moved out over their country as single families or in small groups. A common type of small group was the paired family: two adult brothers, or two sisters, or a brother and sister, with their spouses, small children and perhaps aged parents. The Kutchin equated cousins with brothers and sisters; since a Kutchin spent much of his childhood in the paired family, he grew up as intimately with his cousins as with his own siblings.

Life within a household was intimate indeed, since there was nothing like what we would call privacy. The dwellings of northern Indians included such types as stone-and-moss huts, conical skin teepees, brush shelters – all of them small, crowded and smoky. They might be quite cozy if one may judge by early travellers' accounts.

The most characteristic Kutchin dwelling was a dome-shaped lodge about 20 feet in diameter, made of caribou skins stretched over arched poles, with an open fireplace in the centre and a smokehole above. It was kept shipshape, with a designated place for each piece of equipment. In the paired-family arrangement, each side was generally the domain of one family. The oldest inmates, or honoured guests, had a place at the back, away from the cold drafts at the entrance.

In the winter, camp was moved by sled, but the sleds were not pulled by dogteams, because the subarctic Indians for the most part did not use much dog traction until the establishment of the European fur trade. The few dogs kept by the Kutchin were used mainly for hunting, and for packing in the summer. The sleds were pulled by the women and the older children. Europeans, meeting parties of Indians on the move, concluded that the women were mere beasts of burden. This was not true. What the outsider did not take into account was that the men were at the same time hunting, ranging the country on both sides of the trail, and covering three or four times as much mileage as the women. Women worked very hard, but their position was by no means lowly. A woman had her work and a man his; neither could get along without the other.

Far behind the main party, moving along a trail parallel to it but never on the same trail, there might be an elderly woman, leading a girl who had recently reached puberty. The girl had to be helped and led, because she was wearing a deerskin head covering or cowl that fell in front of her face. This was worn to prevent her gaze falling upon any of the many things which it could harm; for among these people, as among many peoples throughout the world, a girl at puberty was considered to be in a magically dangerous and harmful state. Her glance, or her mere presence, was believed to be especially noxious to things associated with men, such as weapons, and also to young men themselves. Not far up the Peel River from Fort McPherson, Northwest Territories, is a place called Shilti, a formation of three tall rock pillars and a shorter one — two have tumbled down — the remains, it is said, of three brothers and their dog, who were petrified when a girl in this condition carelessly looked out over the landscape and saw them. In camp, the girl lived alone in a small lodge, being cared for by older women. She remained in isolation for six to eight months, being married soon after "coming out." Shortly before puberty, boys left their families and went to live with all the other older boys and unmarried youths of the band. They camped together as a group, directed by skilled mature hunters. The boys were in strict training, kept busy all day, and obliged to subsist on very little food and drink. The training in stamina, running, tracking, and bushcraft would be essential in later life. To this day, the phrases "good runner" and "tough traveller" are terms of high praise to a Kutchin. Although marriages were to some extent arranged between families, the young people — girls as well as boys — had some say in the matter. In any case, early marriages among northern Indians were far from sacrosanct, and were as likely as not to break up. Here again, the woman as well as the man might take the initiative.

The Kutchin had band chiefs. The chieftainship was hereditary, not from father to son, but within a kinship group. The chief did not necessarily exercise a great deal of power by virtue of his office; his authority depended largely upon his personal ability. In this, the Kutchin were again intermediate among northern Indians. To the east of them, leadership was exerted only within the family or a group of closely related families, where there might be a sort of patriarch. Very occasionally, an unusually able and dominant man might appear who attracted a wider following for a time, but his authority was not hereditary, and might not last throughout his lifetime. To the west and south of the Kutchin, there was more stable political organization, with fairly authoritative chieftainship and with a noticeable difference, between some families and others, in heritable wealth.

A chief, like any other effective or outstanding person, had some "medicine," that is, magical power, but there were in addition men, and sometimes women, who had been endowed by the spirits with special powers of clairvoyance, healing, prophecy, and perhaps, power for sorcery or evil magic. In the comparative study of religions, such people are called shamans. Some wonderful tales are told among northern Indians about the performances of shamans, and about contests between shamans. Shaman and Christian missionary were often bitterly opposed, but not always. In some cases, the shaman and his people saw no inconsistency between belief in aboriginal and in Christian doctrine. One of the most powerful of recent Kutchin medicine men, who died around 1920, was also an active lay official in his Christian church.

Life was hard for the northern Indians, but it was not all grim. They were, and still are, passionate gamblers, ardent sportsmen and athletes. Song and dance was valued among them, and especially perhaps, the verbal arts: story-telling, eloquence in public address, and wit in repartee. These arts depend so much upon mastery of the native languages and the possibilities they afford for style and verbal deftness, that very few non-Indians have ever been aware of these accomplishments, still less, able to appreciate them. If this were not so, our image of the dour and taciturn Indian might have been corrected to some extent.

DR. RICHARD SLOBODIN, *Associate Professor, Dept. of Sociology and Anthropology, McMaster University. Born Manhattan, 1915. High school English teacher, New York, 1938. Ph.D., Anthropology, Columbia University, 1959. Research with Kutchin Indians in Fort McPherson region, 1938-39 and 1946-47. Grant from U.S. National Science Foundation used to visit Indian communities in Yukon, 1961. Research on Kutchin of Arctic Red River with grant from National Museum of Canada, 1962. Author of monographs on Kutchin and on the Mackenzie District Metis.*

PROF. JUNE HELM

Changes in Indian Communities

*As opportunities for jobs, goods and services
increase, the Athapaskan Indians
of the north are moving from their isolated
"bush" communities into the
white-dominated settlements. In doing so,
some of the traditional values and
virtues of small-community life may be lost.*

The bush Indian of the Canadian north — who comes to the fort only for trade and Treaty — is disappearing. Especially since World War II, increasing job opportunities and the lure of various Euro-Canadian comforts and services have accelerated the movement of the Indians of the Northwest Territories into the white-centred town as permanent residents in permanent dwellings. For the anthropologist, many of the more traditional modes of social identity and social organization can now be seen only in the small all-Indian settlements in the bush, rather than in the larger communities created and focused around Euro-Canadian institutions.

The bush hamlet of today represents a stabilization of the old fluid, mobile local band. The most visible feature of change is the log cabin dwellings that have replaced the tepee-lodge. These permanent cabins and all the goods and gear from the western world have made present-day Indians relatively less mobile than their ancestors. The bush communities of today are commonly situated along routes of travel, waterways navigable by canoe that lead to the trading fort.

Within the Déné bush village, all members of the community are linked together by multiple ties of blood and marriage. All are kinsmen. The bush community characteristically is created when a man of unusual personality and ability withdraws to settle with his children or his brothers in a new area of the bush. A powerful figure is able not only to maintain the allegiance of his sons and brothers, but to recruit sons-in-law and brothers-in-law to his band. In the past, and to some extent today, the traditional custom of bride service serves as one mode of recruitment to the bush band-community. When a young man marries, he is expected to remain with his bride's group, helping his in-laws, until the birth of the first child. If his father-in-law or one of his brothers-in-law is especially attractive as a good hunter, hard worker, and friend, the young man and his bride are apt to continue to remain in that community rather than to turn to the bridegroom's group.

The smaller bush communities may be composed of only four to eight households. As death brings about the dissolution of the closer ties of kinship, such small local bands may fragment and, in some cases, disappear.

Life in the bush community reveals a prime characteristic of the social organization of the Northern Athapaskan peoples. It is a society by consensus. The diffuse, informal sanctions of gossip, exhortation, ridicule, and public disapproval operate to maintain social order in the absence of any formal or legal mechanisms. The role of the leader in the local band, as of all leaders in the past, is not to enforce physically the unwritten rules of Déné society but, rather to reinforce, by example of his own actions, the basic moral obligations of community life. The principles of autonomy and equality — every man his own boss and every man as good as the next — are deep-seated themes in Déné social life. And in the bush community there still endures a third theme, that of the basic responsibility of each person towards all members of his localized group.

The bush community is small enough that any large game killed, moose or caribou, is shared with all households of the band. And the family whose nets and snares have not yielded enough fish and rabbit for the day may expect to receive a share of a kinsman-neighbour's catch upon request. So, too, borrowing back and forth of European tools and implements and of tea, sugar, and other store staples is continual. As in any small, closely woven, intimate community of human beings, frictions and factions are inevitable. But a sense of social solidarity mediated through kin ties is apparently sufficient to mute and dissolve conflicts before they reach a critical stage. And, if indeed they should, the dissident members can always move to another band or community where they have resident kinsmen.

Two contrapuntal rhythms run through life in a bush band: the daily round of livelihood — fetching water and firewood, tending the nets and snares, all the tasks of maintaining the household; and the seasonal rhythms — the fall fishery, the winter trapline, the spring beaver hunt. For everyone, Sunday is a day of relaxation and in most communities, of a group religious service.

In the simple division of labor in the bush, man provides and woman processes. From the meat, fish and pelts brought by the husband into the household, the wife must prepare dry fish and dry meat, cure moose and caribou hides for moccasins and mitts, flesh and scrape skins for the trader. A man varies his trapping with hunting, and his labour in the bush with trips to the trading fort. For the woman there are only small breaks in household routine — an expedition for berries in the summer with other women and their children, a short social visit on Sunday to the next house, or a few hours spent with a kinswoman while together they do the heavy work of washing and wringing a moosehide. Perhaps only once a year, at Treaty time, does the woman get a visit to the trading fort. But she shares the excitement of all on the return of the men from their trips.

The return of several men from the trapline or from an extended hunt is an occasion for partying and relaxation. Freed from the surveillance of white authority, the bush wife has had no problem in preparing a pot of brew for her husband's return. He and his cronies gather over the pot, each man to tell the tale of his fur take or of the excitement of a moose-kill. Perhaps, from time to time, a cup is also dipped for the ladies present, and the children, enjoying the excitement of the occasion, tear about from cabin to cabin to miss nothing that is going on. Should too much brew release smouldering grudges, the women and near kinsmen are ready to lead potential combatants away to their own homes. The brew party serves to break the monotony of toil and isolation. The slow evolution of a brew party, as the alcohol in the sweet cidery drink begins to take hold, allows a change of social and emotional pace that, in one way or another, all cultures of the world have institutionalized to accommodate the nature of the human animal. The more frenetic pace of partying that hard liquor now allows Indian as well as white in the north does not seem as satisfactory, as anyone who has tried to pace himself at a martini party will admit.

The physical convenience, the economic and educational opportunities of the white-centred community will surely in the future more and more dissolve the ties of the Northern Déné to the bush environment. To the Indian of today the rigors of bush living may be too great a price to pay for the more independent and self-sufficient life of his forbears. The bush village imposes isolation upon the Indian and economic bondage to the vagaries of the fur trade. Yet by standards common to both Indian and white — the equalitarian relationships within the community, and the almost complete absence of crime, psychosis, broken homes, abandoned wives and children — the Athapaskan bush community is a very healthy social body. Many southern Canadian and United States tribes are not so fortunate.

PROF. JUNE HELM, *Associate Professor, Anthropology, University of Iowa. M.A., Ph.D., University of Chicago. Field work among the Déné or Athapaskan peoples of Mackenzie Drainage in Northwest Territories, including Slavey, Hare and Dogrib. Lectured ten years at Carleton University, Ottawa, and summer school of University of Manitoba. Editor of publications of American Ethnological Society, member editorial council of American Anthropological Association, consulting director Canadian Research Centre for Anthropology.*

PROF. VIC VALENTINE

The Forgotten People

The Metis are neither Indian, Eskimo nor white.
No federal or provincial agency
is legally charged with their welfare; they
might even be called "The Unknown People."

The early history of the Northwest is filled with reference to a group of people who have been referred to variously as *half-breeds, breeds, voyagers, bois-brûles* or *Metis*. They were the descendants of Indian mothers and European fathers. Their mothers came from great tribes of the plains and forestlands: Cree, Sowto, Blackfoot, Chipewyan, Dogrib and Slavey to mention a few. Their fathers were immigrant settlers and employees of the fur trading companies, and came mainly from France and Scotland. No one knows how many of these people there are in Canada, or for that matter, how to distinguish or define them as a group. It used to be popular to say that mister so-and-so was a full-blooded Indian or mister such-and-such was half, quarter or eighth blood. We know now that blood has nothing to do with inheritance of physical or mental characteristics, and to refer to people in this way is erroneous. The carriers of inheritable characteristics are the genes, which are found in the chromosomes of the female ova and the male sperm.

In 1951, when the present Indian Act was revised, this fact was recognized and the definition of an Indian changed from "any male person of Indian blood . . ." to "a person who pursuant to this Act, is registered as an Indian or is entitled to be registered." The terms, half-breed or breed, once fashionable are, because of the change in the Act, not accurate anymore in referring to this group. The French word "Metis" is much preferred, not only because it is less invidious sounding, but because it more accurately reflects the situation as it implies simply "mixed descent."

Metis are not, constitutionally speaking, Indians; that is, they do not come under the Indian Act, and therefore do not have the special rights and responsibilities as outlined in the Act. They are the responsibilities of the provinces, as are other citizens. As a matter of fact, it is only in the western provinces and the Northwest Territories that they seem to be recognized, at least semi-officially. This is probably due to the role they played in the history of the west, particularly in the Riel rebellion of 1870 and 1885. The relatively small population in these areas makes them stand out more readily and recognizably as a group. More and more, they are being viewed by the governments as a distinct group in need of special assistance. The provinces of Alberta, Saskatchewan and Manitoba are now implementing special programs.

Yet, it remains difficult to say who is and who is not a Metis. In the early days of the Red River Settlement, according to the census of 1870 or '71, there were over 10,000 people in the vicinity of this settlement; of these, some 1,200 were classified as whites and the remainder as Metis of Scotch-Indian or French-Indian descent. The costume worn by both white and Metis groups was much the same, except that a red sash was worn around the waist over one's coat among the white group, and under the coat among the Metis group. The Metis lived mainly as buffalo hunters; few were interested in the sedentary life based on agriculture. Many resented the coming of the farmer and the railroad, because they restricted the growth and movement of the buffalo herds, thus jeopardizing their main source of food and income.

The range of physical characteristics among the group which identifies itself as Metis covers the whole spectrum from white-skinned, blue-eyed blond individuals to those with typical Indian characteristics of bronze-coloured skins, dark eyes and hair, and facial structure. It is a case where appearance alone is deceiving. Indeed the same holds true for Treaty Indians, and it is doubtful whether there is, from a biological point of view, a 100 per cent true-blue Indian left in Canada. Probably the best definition I have heard in answer to the question, "What is a Metis?" was given to me by an old Metis man of northern Saskatchewan, who said, "A

Metis is a man who, when he has no money, lives like an Indian, and when he has money lives like a white man."

While the definition stresses the economic condition of an individual, more than this is implied. What distinguishes a Metis group from Indians or whites are social and psychological problems. These are not often obvious to someone who encounters a Metis group for the first time. In the northern part of the prairie provinces and in the Northwest Territories, it is estimated that the Metis make up about one-third of the total population. For the greater part, they are descendants of French and Scottish ancestors who worked for the Hudson's Bay Company or the old North West Company. Old Scottish and French surnames still identify them, and such names as Isbester, Mackay, and Ross or La Liberte and Desjarlais are much in evidence.

In the early days, they worked for the company as porters, canoe-men and builders. They lived in small settlements along the great waterways of the north. With the decline in the fur trade and the coming of the railroads and highways, they lost their jobs as transporters and builders. Although they remained in the north, they became like their Indian ancestors, hunters and trappers, and acting frequently in their historic role as interpreters, as well as go-betweens for Indians and whites.

In the area with which I am most familiar — northern Saskatchewan — they now live in small semi-isolated settlements of about 300 people clustered around the store, mission and government outpost. Some of these settlements were once well-known names to all Canadians during the early part of the last century: Ile-à-la-Crosse, where Louis Riel was born, and where the first hospital in western Canada was built; Portage La Loche, where a 12-mile portage separates the Churchill River system from the Mackenzie River system, and where it is said over 80 per cent of the fur wealth in Canada at one time passed. Curiously, the majority of the Metis on the west side of the province have French surnames, and on the east side, Scottish. This is probably due to the influence of the Hudson's Bay Company on the east side before 1820, and the Montreal-based North West Company on the west side of the province.

Perhaps because they were raised by Indian mothers, the bush Metis learned more about Indian ways than they did white ways. Their first language was an Indian dialect, and they developed a preference for Indian food. Yet many of their customs and even language reflect white influence. The Cree-speaking Metis of northern Saskatchewan for example, use many French words, particularly nouns, so the language is neither pure Cree nor pure French. In the method of raising children and making a living, the Indian pattern is frequently followed, particularly with regard to the organization of family life, naming of kindred, and sharing among kin of possessions and food. In some ways, they have remained more like the traditional Indian of the area in mode of living, because they have not been restricted by the terms of the treaties or the Indian Act. Generally, compared to southern standards they are poor. Those who live by hunting and trapping make less than a thousand dollars per year. Their homes are usually one-room log cabins, sparsely furnished. Few have progressed beyond the elementary grades. Yet, anyone who has met them will find them hardy, hospitable, and full of good humour. Some writers have referred to them as a "marginal" people, since they are not accepted by either white or Indian groups. I do not like the term and seldom use it, for I believe there is far more interchange and contact among the groups than meets the eye or ear of the casual observer.

Whatever the case, the plight or condition of the Metis will always be a measure of how successful we, as a nation, are in bringing to them the benefits of modern civilization. They represent not only culturally, but biologically, a transitional step between the different cultures. As long as there are Indians, and as long as there is the so-called Indian problem, there will be Metis and a Metis problem, for the process of marriage and inter-mixture among the groups is still going on.

According to the Indian Act, a person is entitled to be registered as an Indian when the father was an Indian, as defined by the Act. This means that, if a white or Metis man marries an Indian woman, their children cannot be registered as Indian. But if a Metis or white woman marries an Indian man, their children can be registered as Indian. As the majority of mixed marriages are between white men and Indian women, the Metis population grows by addition as well as by natural increase. The confusion which such legal distinctions make in the everyday life of both people or of the extraordinary administrative complications which ensue, are beyond comprehension.

PROF. VIC VALENTINE, *Associate Professor of Sociology, Carleton University. War service in R.C.N. Honours in Anthropology, University of Toronto, 1951; M.A., Anthropology, University of Toronto, 1952. Study of Metis people. Mary Jean Felkner award, 1953. Director of Research, Dept. of Natural Resources, Saskatchewan; Chief, Northern Co-ordination and Research Centre, Dept. of Northern Affairs and National Resources; Chief, Economic Development Division, Indian Affairs Branch, 1964-65.*

DR. DAVID DAMAS

Eskimo Communities then and now

*A nomadic people adapts to life in stable
settlements where the sharp impact of
two cultures brings new challenges to both the
Eskimo and to the agents
of modern Canadian society.*

Contact with Europeans has brought about marked changes in Eskimo communities. In order to gain some understanding of changing Eskimo communities it would be appropriate to consider them as they appeared during each of three stages of Eskimo history: 1. the aboriginal, 2. the contact-traditional, and 3. the centralized.

During the early historical period the Eskimo met mainly with whalers and exploratory parties. The traditional technology, economy, ideology, and social organization remained intact. Eskimo community organization in this still aboriginal period fell into two categories: the permanent settlements of Alaska and Greenland and the highly nomadic groups of snowhouse and tent-dwelling Central Eskimo. I will focus my remarks on the latter groups.

The aboriginal Central Eskimo groups followed a uniform pattern of combining and splitting which was harmonious with the seasonal hunting cycle. Groups averaging about 100 individuals gathered on the sea ice in winter for breathing-hole sealing. These gatherings, which lasted for periods of up to five months, represented the annual assemblages of Central Eskimo bands. Each band split into hunting groups of 5 to 50 persons during the remainder of the year when the economy shifted variously to caribou hunting, fishing and sea mammal hunting from kayaks.

The winter band assemblage and the summer hunting groups were made up of face-to-face groups of people connected by ties of kinship. Kinship formed the basis for much personal interaction and established strong emotional bonds within the community. Marriage, adoption and naming were also regulated according to kinship factors. In some regions the primary family consisting of parents and unmarried children comprised the chief household unit and the unit within which meat was distributed. Elsewhere, the extended family which included married children made up these units. At Igloolik, and probably further east as well, a formal leader was recognized over the entire band. Elsewhere, community organization was democratic and decisions were made by consensus.

The network of kinship relationships meshed with a network of voluntary partnerships such as those relating to meat sharing, spouse exchange, joking and dancing, so that each community was cross-hatched by a series of internal bonds.

Social control revolved around use of public ridicule, insult singing contest, fisticuffs and even occasional execution after group agreement on the matter. Withdrawal to other bands was a common means of resolving frictions. Other reasons for movement among bands were the wish to exploit new hunting areas, periodic visiting of relatives, and trade. This movement was generally restricted within a group of five or six bands. Nearly all of the marriages were contracted within this cluster of bands which can be called the tribe.

The winter band assemblage provided opportunity for dances, athletic contests, and performances by shamans. The tribe, even though it never formed a single local group, comprised a body of people who spoke a common dialect, shared the same customs and were linked by ties of kinship. Each tribe was set off rather sharply from its neighbours in each of these ways.

The aboriginal communities of the summer hunting groups and the winter band aggregation comprised groups which were generally harmonious aggregates of people and which were well fitted to the task of making a living off the land. This adaptation, both external and internal, was based on traditional social customs. The aboriginal period ended between 1900 and 1925 (depending on the region) with the appearance of fur traders, missionaries, and police who ushered in the contact-traditional phase of Eskimo history. With the introduction of the steel trap, the net, and the rifle, new hunting techniques were used and it was no longer necessary for the Eskimo to gather in the large sealing village. The trapping-hunting camp became the typical settlement. This camp was a permanent version of the small aboriginal summer hunting group. The focus of travel and the centre of contact now shifted to the trading post. The trading community was usually made up of the members of one or two bands. Occasionally, the entire trading group would converge at the post but these were short-termed gatherings, since the traders did not encourage the Eskimo to live around the post. Though their importance faded slowly in the more remote areas, the wider aspects of kinship and the voluntary associations largely disappeared along with the traditional band assemblage. In short, the organization of the Central Eskimo into nomadic bands died during the contact-traditional period. The tribe, too, lost much of its aboriginal character. Since the highly nomadic hunting groups of the earlier periods had been replaced by the much more stationary trapping-hunting camp, which related chiefly to the post, contacts within the wider tribal area became fewer. Identification of the group centred on the post. For example, the Copper Eskimo tribe of the aboriginal period became the Perry River people, the Bathurst Inlet people, and the Coppermine people.

Traders, missionaries, and police exercised paternalistic supervision over economic, religious and legal life, but the day-to-day life decisions were still left largely in Eskimo hands, since most settlements continued as all-native establishments. Family organization persisted much as before and close-knit kin ties continued to be important. Hunting, trapping and meat sharing were sometimes individualistic but more often were organized within the extended family or on a camp-wide basis.

The actions of the police replaced native legal sanctions, to a large extent, though the traditional means of settling conflicts through withdrawal to other groups remained important. Christianity affected the spiritual life of the Eskimo but his view of the universe was still mainly determined by traditional beliefs regarding the supernatural.

Over a 30- or 40-year period the contact-traditional camp community grew to be a more or less stabilized type of organization. It represented an adjustment to a changed economy and to culture contact but its basic organization was rooted in the heritage of aboriginal Eskimo society. Eskimo community life appears to have lost some of its vitality due to the break-up of the band organization and the weakening of wider tribal bonds.

The contact-traditional type camp still survives but it is being rapidly replaced by the large mixed Eskimo-white settlements that developed at the centres of Euro-Canadian activity in the north — places like Cambridge Bay and Frobisher Bay. These settlements represent the third or centralized phase of the history of Eskimo communities.

Centralization of Eskimo populations at such communities usually stemmed from multiple causes. Primarily these were inability of the Eskimo to live off the game of the country, plus the opportunities for wage labour, the presence of schools, government aid programs, and the related motive of seeking the more exciting life offered by the centralized community.

In their inception the native sections of the centralized mixed communities were made up of a group of all-native camps which formed separate neighbourhoods. Some of the large centralized communities included people from different trading areas or even different tribal areas. The overall native community thus comprised a formless gathering of people and did not constitute an actual society held together by internal organization.

More recently with the introduction of modern housing, division of the community into these neighbourhoods has begun to break-down. The scope of kinship has begun to grow through inter-marriages between members of groups who had come from different regions. One may wonder, however, whether kinship will ever provide the chief means of achieving social integration. Differences in income, occupational status, and level of education may promote an incipient class structure similar to that of Euro-Canadian society.

The control of most decision-making by white agencies deprives the Eskimo community of self-sufficiency in social organization. A general lack of local resources and industries keep the Eskimo dependent upon goods from the outside. Purchase of these goods is often impossible because of the lack of opportunities for earning cash income.

Culture change in the contact-traditional period was most marked in technology. One of the results of the access to education and mass media that is available in the centralized communities may well be dramatic changes in Eskimo views of the world and in his system of values.

Contrasted with the communities of the earlier stages of Eskimo history the centralized mixed communities lack economic self-sufficiency and internal unity. In addition, the impact of foreign culture that confronts the Eskimo of these communities is the most powerful and pervasive in Eskimo history.

DR. DAVID DAMAS, *National Museum of Canada. Born Wisconsin, 1926. B.A., University of Toledo, 1950. M.A., University of Chicago, 1960. Ph.D., 1962. Several field trips to the Eskimo. Igloolik, 1960-61; Bathurst Inlet, Perry River, Cambridge Bay, 1962-63; Gjoa Haven and Spence Bay, 1965.*

PROF. NELSON GRABURN

Mixed Communities

*The 20th century produced the phenomenon
of mixed communities in
the north. But to what extent do the
races actually mix?*

Mixed communities are those in which members of the population
have two or more considerably different cultural backgrounds or,
in other terms, belong to at least two different ethnic groups. They
may be called multi-ethnic communities. Nearly all communities
in the Canadian north are today multi-ethnic, mainly because the
white man has penetrated or "colonized" nearly all those areas previously inhabited by either Eskimos or Indians. In this chapter I
would like to limit my remarks to those communities in which considerable proportions of the population come from different ethnic
groups.

While multi-ethnic communities are found all through the north
and range in size from large cities like Churchill to the smallest
DEW Line sites, my experiences have been mainly in the eastern
arctic with medium-sized communities that might be thought of as
small towns or large villages. In the north, these mixed communities share one important characteristic. Their very existence is, in
every case, the result of the activities of the white man in the area.
The Canadian north, unlike many other areas of the world, did not
originally have any mixed communities. As is well known, the
Indians and the Eskimos everywhere avoided each other except for
hostile military contacts, and, for the most part, the various different Indian groups kept away from each other. Before the coming of
the white man, typical Eskimo and Indian communities were small,

family-based, temporary, and culturally homogeneous. Mixed communities, then, are the creations of the white man.

With the variety of cultural groups in the north — white, Eskimo, and different groups of Indians — there are various combinations in these mixed communities. Some of these have just Eskimos and whites together, such as Frobisher Bay. Further south, more subarctic than arctic, other communities have only white and Indian groups. I do not wish to consider those many smaller communities where there are a few whites associated with a large majority of natives. I do not use the word "native" in any derogatory sense. I mean simply "those born there," which for the most part includes just Eskimos and Indians. The white men in the area are rarely permanent residents and it is the theme of this chapter to demonstrate that the permanent native Eskimos and Indians are fast becoming one lower caste group as opposed to the temporary but dominant whites.

Across the arctic we find a number of communities, some quite old, with all three groups, white, Indian and Eskimo. These present more complicated problems than those with only two groups. It is quite significant that there are no communities which are only Eskimo and Indian, showing again that the white man is the catalyst for cultural heterogeneity. For instance, the Eskimos and Indians of Great Whale River and, formerly, Fort Chimo would never have lived together without the encouraging and moderating presence of the white man. Another case, we should not forget, are communities containing two different Indian groups along with the white man; groups that would not be there without the white man's presence. Churchill is one example. Another is Knob Lake, or Schefferville, where the author spent a month in the spring of 1964.

In the latter case the two Indian groups, known by the whites as "Naskapi" and "Montagnais," have settled there in large numbers since the formation of the iron ore mining town in 1953. Here the Indians form a mixed community more through white influences than native differences. To the Indians there was very little difference between the wandering bands of the northern Naskapi and the Montagnais to the south. They were all Indians "iijuts." However, the Naskapi fell under the influence of Anglican English-speaking whites, whereas the Montagnais along the St. Lawrence River were converted to Catholicism and many have learned to speak French. Although the original languages of the two groups were mutually intelligible, with their new loyalties the two groups find themselves more different and less able to communicate than they did, say 100 years ago. This is a somewhat "artificial" division between two previously fairly similar groups, a division which is already beginning to break down because of the relatively smaller numbers of Naskapi and the pressures where both groups are similarly subject to the omnipotent white powers.

Although the John Lake Reservation is technically only for the Naskapi, the Montagnais, whose "home" is Seven Islands, Que., are present as "squatters" in considerably larger number. For this and other reasons, more than half the marriages contracted by the Naskapi since 1956 have been with Montagnais. Not only does this tend to create an undifferentiated "Indian" group, but, because of the relatively fewer numbers of Naskapi, they may very well disappear altogether as an independent group.

If, before the coming of the white man, the people of the various ethnic groups never got together and formed mixed communities, how and why did these come about? In the past, the usual reason was the advent of the trader. The white traders went into the subarctic and arctic to trade for the valuable furs of the area, caring little whether they got them from Eskimos or Indians. The Indians, of course, had traded with the white man long before the Eskimos and it was only in the last century that trading posts were started at the northern edge of the subarctic, that is, close enough to the treeline to attract Eskimos. The latter, too, wished to partake of the material advantages of this trade like their enemies the Indians. Neither of these groups wished in any way to assimilate to white culture, at least in those days; rather, both groups wanted the new goods, particularly metal objects and guns, in order to pursue more efficiently their traditional hunting activities. Typical were Great Whale River and Fort Chimo, both near the boundary between the traditionally hostile Eskimos and Indians. The desire to trade for white goods overcame some of these feelings. Some of the white traders would only trade with either group on condition they did not use the new weapons to continue their warlike practices. Thus these two communities, like many others in the southern arctic, became special-purpose communities where the two native groups would make occasional contact incidental to their trading activities. Neither group lived permanently in the settlements and they maintained their mutual avoidance as much as possible.

A very good description of the traditional attitudes and hostilities between the Indians and Eskimos is given by the novelist R. M. Ballantyne in his novel *Ungava* (1857) in which he describes the difficulties the Hudson's Bay Company had in trying to open up the trading post at Fort Chimo and thereby create a mixed community of Eskimos and Naskapi Indians.

Considerably later, the missionaries had a further salutary influence. Conversion to Christianity, with its emphasis on non-violence and "loving thine enemy" further allayed the hostilities of the native groups. During the earlier part of this century both groups began to feel secure enough to live in the same regions. Still, contacts were neither constant nor intimate. For instance, in Fort Chimo the two groups made their camps on opposite sides of the trading post about half a mile apart. A particularly vivid account of the hostile and suspicious relationship between the Eskimos and the Naskapi Indians at Fort Chimo at the beginning of this century is given by Anauta, the Eskimo wife of the white trader Harry Ford. What the two groups had in common was the result of their similar white contacts: their religion, their hunting and trapping tools, and their introductions to the white economy and society.

More recently, other types of mixed communities have developed in the north, stemming from World War II and the postwar period with the air bases and the various radar sites. Frobisher Bay is a good example. Though there had been a trader there since early this century, it was not until the 'forties and 'fifties that the opening of the radar and air bases attracted Eskimos in very large numbers. In this case, the promises of jobs, better housing, and variety of white agencies attracted the Eskimos to the already burgeoning white community.

In all these mixed communities the groups with different cultural backgrounds kept themselves apart, although they lived reasonably close together. Similar situations often developed with the various immigrant groups in the United States and Canada.

However, in some of the more acculturated communities things have begun to change. In many places the main obvious division has become that between the whites and the native groups, Indian and/or Eskimo. There has developed a caste-like relationship between whites and natives. Each of the two groups live very different kinds of lives, with different occupational niches, seeing their situations in very different ways. Both the Eskimos and Indians have almost identical relationships to the white "powers." Where, in some places, the Eskimos and Indians find themselves in this "lower caste," many have forgotten, at least consciously, their hostilities and differences. On the other hand, in some places considerable hostilities, both overt and covert, have developed between the native "lower caste" and the white "upper caste." This is particularly true in the Mackenzie Delta, especially in the acculturated communities of Inuvik and Aklavik. It is also beginning to be obvious in the larger eastern arctic communities. Without further great changes in mutual attitudes, the outcome will be a series of divided caste-communities with the dominant whites trying to live a middle class life in surroundings which few whites consider congenial and permanent, and a lower caste of natives, Indian or Eskimo or both, living their own different lower caste life, dependent on the whites and mainly engaged in lower echelon employment. Because the majority of whites are not permanently in the north, and most are working for the high wages and savings, early retirement, or transfer to Ottawa, it is difficult to see much further assimilation between the native and white groups. Perhaps in those few places which numbers of whites come to regard as "home" there will be a breakdown of the economic and social barriers, but for most places this is in the far distant future.

Mixed communities are subject to problems, some common to all native arctic communities, some special to multi-ethnic situations. First, it should not be forgotten that the white people in the north are not "ordinary" Canadians or Europeans. They are specialists, either in technical fields such as mechanics or teachers, or in dealing with the natives, such as Indian and Eskimo agents, traders, and missionaries. The natives are ordinary, non-specialists in their own homeland. All of them have to deal with the vicissitudes of their environment and the white man, not just those few who choose to go north.

In the past, many of the special problems stemmed partly from the hostility between the various cultures. Although Eskimos and Indians both wanted to trade with the white man and get his goods, they did not particularly want to have anything to do with each other. Originally they didn't visit each other, make friends or intermarry. Beyond this was the language barrier, which further hampered most social contacts. In a few places some learned each others' languages, but these were exceptions. Only with universal elementary education in English will the language barrier come down. This will, in turn, aid the formation of the undifferentiated "native lower caste" as well as facilitating better communication with those whites who allow it. In addition, multi-ethnic communities at present have the administrative problem of multiple interpreters enhancing jealousy and mutual suspicion between the two groups trying to curry the white man's favor.

Among the "white upper caste" there are problems of prejudice. Whites often hold strong opinions about the superiority of one or the other of the native groups in some or all of their activities. This often influences their treatment of the two native groups and thus promotes mutual jealousy. While the majority of whites in and out of the north presently admire the Eskimos, there are also those who admire the Indians for their greater discipline and leadership abilities in contrast with the Eskimo's supposed individualism.

A related problem is that in some areas the two native groups live together but are under the control of different white agencies. For instance, the Eskimos at Great Whale River envy the Indians' larger and more substantial houses, whereas the Indians envy the Eskimos' multitude of agencies and apparent favour with the whites. At this stage of acculturation the cultural differences and reactions of the two groups are marked. The Eskimos cling to their new religion and white assistance and look upon the past as "the bad old days." The Indians, who feel themselves to be the underdogs, see the past as the "good old days" when they were freer and had superior supernatural powers which the white man has somehow stolen from them. With further acculturation and education a new stage will be reached where the Eskimos and Indians will submerge most of their differences, learn more of each other's ways and feel themselves in the same boat as against the ever-powerful white man. I am told by a number of my anthropologist friends, especially Mr. Ernie Burch and Mrs. Nancy Davis, that a similar situation is also present in parts of Alaska; so these problems are by no means unique to Canada!

Typically, in the larger communities drinking has become a problem. Sometimes it brings to violence the latent antagonism between the native groups and at a later stage between the natives and the whites. Because of their different backgrounds the reactions of Indians and Eskimos to drink differ, but will soon cease to do so. At present with Indians, drunkenness tends to violence, even against family and friends, whereas Eskimos tend more easily to turn to sex or sleep. The latter unfortunately has led to death for those unable to reach home on winter nights, as happened at Frobisher Bay in the winter of 1963-64.

Similarly, where there is a demand for prostitution there is a willing supply, especially where there is drinking, although it is more usual with the more outgoing Eskimo women. Indian women, too, are breaking with their former discipline and, like the Eskimos, overcome their scruples where there is material advantage or prestige available. Neither of these problems are particularly peculiar to the north or multi-ethnic communities, but both are entirely the result of white contact.

To summarize, the problem is inevitably one of power. The overall tendency is for all native groups to be treated similarly by the contact agencies, stores, schools, police, etc., and in some places both Indians and Eskimos are represented on rather important councils and even co-operatives. These native power elites have little in common with the white powers who actually run things. The effect of all this is to merge the native groups, leading to a series of highly polarized communities of opposing dominant whites and dependent natives. As in caste situations all over the world, the two groups have their own ways of life, their own appointed and hereditary tasks, their own views of themselves and each other, a feeling of resentment of those who associate with the opposite group and a tendency of the men of the "higher" group to have sexual access to the women of the "lower" group, but not vice versa.

One perceptive white official who has had experience in many parts of the arctic, but now works in Ottawa, has said that under present conditions the native groups of the arctic will become united as the "oil barrel rollers" and will long remain so. He saw the only alternative to this caste-like situation as the gathering of the "backward" groups in a very few large centres where they could quickly be acculturated towards the Euro-Canadian way of life and become educationally equipped to compete in the majority society. We, as observers and participants in this unfolding story, hope that the problems can be alleviated without such drastic measures, which might, in effect, wipe out the remnants of these hardy Indian and Eskimo cultures, turning their members into menial components of the lowest class of our own socio-economic hierarchy. We can only work and wait.

PROF. NELSON GRABURN, *Assistant Professor, Anthropology, University of California, Berkeley, California. B.A., Anthropology and Natural Sciences, Cambridge, 1958; M.A., McGill University, 1960; Ph.D., University of Chicago, 1963. Field work: among the Eskimos of Sugluk, Que. and along the south coast of the Hudson Strait; among the Eskimos of Lake Harbour and Frobisher Bay, Baffin Island, N.W.T.; among the Eskimos and Indians of the Ungava Peninsula through all communities from Fort Chimo to Inuvik then to Schefferville, Povungnituk and Great Whale River; for the Cooperative Cross-cultural Study of Ethnocentrism, Northwestern University, Evanston, Illinois, U.S.A., 1963-64.*

DR. CHARLES HOBART

Local Schools versus Hostels

*What is the solution to the problem of
educating children in the sparsely settled
north: large hostels creating
a sustained separation from the family or a
teacher in every community however small.*

There are many problems in providing schooling for the children of northern Canada. One difficulty is the fact that children are often widely scattered over large areas, but money can provide a ready solution to the problem and during the last decade the government has provided funds generously.

But money cannot supply answers to other questions. Should children be enabled to go to school as long as possible in their home settlements so that their parents may train them in conduct and conscience, and teach them the lore of living on the land? Or should they leave home early, perhaps when they enter school, in order to learn the middle-class, white, city people ways of the south, by living in residences and going to classrooms like those of the south? Should one worry about educating the child to dissatisfaction with his home, his parents, his community, so that he cannot really go home again, after his education is finished? Or is preparing him to make the most of the opportunities that may come his way the only thing that really matters?

Should he have the opportunity to learn some of the literature and lore of his own people in school, to learn the native version of the history of the Northwest Territories, for example, rather than the white man's version? Is it discriminatory against northern people not to give their children the same education as every other Canadian child receives? Or is it discriminatory against their language, values and ways of life not to give their children an education which teaches them to know and respect the history and culture of their own people? These are important issues. The way they are decided will greatly affect the lives of thousands of northern children and the histories of the settlements and bands from which they come.

The Danes have faced these same problems in Greenland for almost 200 years. Their solution up until about 10 years ago was simple. They established schools in even the smallest of settlements in which children were taught by the best person available, whether or not he had had any teacher training. Instruction was in the Eskimo language and so were the books which were used. The subject matter taught was chosen to help people to a better living where they were, and included training in handicrafts and hunting skills by the best native hunters. But it was *not* designed to prepare them for life elsewhere. The Danes did not want to prepare them for life elsewhere. The Danes did not want to prepare people for jobs which might not exist; they did not try to teach a *Danish* way of life.

For almost 200 years the Eskimos were taught in this manner, were well prepared to live their lives and were content. But about 10 years ago, the Danes woke up, perhaps a little late, to the changes that had come with World War II. To prepare Eskimos for today's and tomorrow's world they have now brought in 300 Danish teachers to teach in Greenland. They have published a special series of school books for Greenland, printed in Danish and Eskimo. They have begun to use Danish as the language of instruction in some places, and they send gifted children as young as 10 years old from small settlements to cottage-hostel schools.

There are, of course, some negative reactions to these very sudden changes. Some parents are bewildered. Many native teachers are bitter when they find themselves suddenly placed under Danish teachers, who are usually younger, with much less teaching experience than themselves. Some Greenlanders are protesting the changes as a threat to the survival of their language and culture.

In Alaska the Americans have had schools for northern peoples for 80 years. Day schools were built in many settlements at an early date, and this day school approach was reinforced by the publication of the Merriam Report of 1929. This report was bitterly critical of what happened to Indian children who were taught in residential schools. As a result, day schools have been built where the first grades were taught in every place where 12 or more children could be brought together. Teaching is in English and almost all the books are those used in other states of the Union, a practise that teachers criticize and which officials hope to change within the next few years. The teachers have often been native teaching aides who had some training but did not have full teaching certificates. Children go away to residential school usually only after completing grade eight at home. Still, educational officials are uneasy about sending even high school children away, so strong is their conviction that children should grow up within the home.

Systematic provision for the education of *all* northern Canadian children is very recent, only about 10 years old. The current Canadian program makes fewer concessions to the climate and cultures of the north than either the Danish or the American programs. Instruction is in English, all text books are in English, and in almost every case they were written for southern Canadian children and make use of southern examples, which northern children often cannot understand.

With a few exceptions the teachers are southern Canadians who go north to teach for two or three years without training or experience in teaching northern children. No attempt has been made to give special training to bright native people, who know the north, to see if they might do a better job teaching northern children than transient white teachers.

A high proportion of the children do go to residential schools; in the Mackenzie District about half of all the grade school children are in residential schools, and many have been there since grade one. Curiously the federal government apparently has no consistent policy concerning hostels: in the eastern arctic, hostels are more rare, and they are usually cottage-hostels for children living in the vicinity. In such hostels 10 or 15 children are cared for and supervised by an Eskimo house mother. In the Mackenzie District children are often taken hundreds of miles to live in large hostels, housing between 100 and 300 children. In these large institutions, the children eat southern Canadian food, have supervisors who are usually southern Canadians, and live under southern standards of warmth, comfort and cleanliness.

The change from the tent or cabin to the large two-storey hostel, and back again, is a drastic one for children in the western arctic. How does this change affect them? I have talked with more than 200 people in the delta and on the arctic coast about this question. Some things are clear. The children *are* frequently homesick. But they hide it from their teachers and supervisors, often because their parents have told them to, and they do handle their homesickness much better than white children would. Many of them find that returning from the comforts of the school to homes which are much smaller, colder, and less clean, is a difficult experience. Parents report that they are "cranky:" they whine and complain and fight more than usual, they are less helpful around the house. But most of them adjust rather fast.

The parents usually feel that these difficulties are unavoidable. Some of them are happy that their children get better food, warmer clothing and better medical care at school than they would at home. Some feel that children learn faster in residential schools. Some are troubled that they cannot teach their children what they should know to be able to live off the land. Teachers are usually troubled that the children are away from their mothers and families, but some feel that the hostel children miss less school and are less often sleepy in class.

What can we say about the results of the system? Very little so far. On the one hand, there are young people from the north in several provincial universities, who would not be there were it not for the school system I have described. And on the other hand, there are unhappy, useless, and troublesome young people in some northern settlements who cannot go back to life on the land after living the easy life of the residential school, but who cannot provide for themselves in town either. These two extremes dramatize the problems of northern education. In the years ahead, as more self-government comes to the Territories, northern people will increasingly have to help to find the best solutions.

DR. CHARLES HOBART, *Associate Professor of Sociology, University of Alberta. Born Swatow, China, 1926. B.A., University of Redlands, 1950; M.A., University of California, 1951; Ph.D., Indiana University, 1955. Field work in Canadian arctic and Alaska. Studied the education of native people in Greenland, 1965.*

DR. PERCY MOORE

The Modern Medicine Man

The need for "the modern medicine man"
was obvious once it was realized that native
peoples did not have "acquired immunity"
to many of white man's diseases.

Modern medicine came to the northern peoples through the same
channels which brought other influences to modify their way of
life. It came along the travel routes, brought by the travellers:
whalers, prospectors, fur traders, policemen, missionaries.

The first hospitals were built by the missionaries, and were
located along the Mackenzie River in the western arctic: at Aklavik, Fort Norman, Fort Simpson, Fort Smith, Fort Rae, and Fort
Resolution. The central arctic was served by the hospital at Chesterfield Inlet, and the eastern arctic by the Pangnirtung hospital.

The department of the interior, the department of Indian affairs
and later (after 1935) the appropriate branch of the department of
mines and resources, employed medical officers at these hospitals.

Opening of the mines at Yellowknife brought hospital and medical services there, and of course, the annual Eastern Arctic Patrol
had a doctor in the party. As the available medical care followed
the established routes, only the people along these routes received
medical care. For other communities, medical supplies and advice
were made available to missionaries, trading post personnel, and
the R.C.M.P., all of whom rendered valiant service, and whose
intervention many times meant the difference between life and
death. The advent of generalized modern medical practice had to
await modern communications facilities such as the bush aircraft,
on pontoons or skis, and the two-way radio.

During the war years, if no other medical personnel was available, The Canadian Medical Procurement and Assignment Board seconded national defence medical officers to some of the existing northern hospitals. After the war, during the late 'forties, and since, a steady expansion of facilities has occurred.

In 1955, northern health service was established by a cabinet directive, and the department of national health and welfare by agreement became the health department for the Northwest Territories. It was faced with the tremendous task of extending curative and preventive medical services for a population of some 40,000 people — the population of a medium-sized southern Canadian city — scattered over a million and a half square miles of some of the most desolate and difficult terrain in the world.

Add to this the fact that the white man sometimes brought with him, not only cures for diseases, but new diseases which proved tragically threatening to people who did not have an acquired immunity to them. In the late 'forties, military manoeuvres were held around Fort Chimo. These included a paratroop capture of an air field. Eskimos and their dog teams were employed. Someone brought in a case of measles. The Eskimos left for their homes in the north, up Ungava Bay to George River and Payne Bay, and spread measles to all the camps. One-third of the population died before messages got to the outside and help was flown in.

In the early 'fifties, an Eskimo from Eskimo Point was in contact with a case of poliomyelitis at Churchill. He travelled north to Eskimo Point, and from there, another Eskimo, a special R.C.M.P. constable, went inland to Padlei; at the same time a Roman Catholic priest travelled to Chesterfield Inlet. In both places polio developed. At Chesterfield, 85 per cent of the total population was stricken, with one-third either dying or developing severe paralysis. To add to the tragedy, an R.C.A.F. Canso carrying 21 cases of paralysed people to Winnipeg for special treatment, crashed in northern Manitoba. All were killed, including the crew, and a physiotherapist from Brockville, Ontario, who had volunteered to go to Chesterfield Inlet to work with the victims of paralysis.

A third epidemic occurred at Eskimo Point in 1962 where a single case of TB touched off a rash of almost 90 cases requiring hospital treatment out of a population of slightly over 300.

These three dramatic episodes point up some of northern Canada's health problems.

The Health Service in the north carries on with the work of its predecessors, and can boast some notable achievements. There is now a network of more than 25 nursing stations and health centres, two departmental hospitals (Inuvik and Frobisher) and seven mission hospitals, backed up by base hospitals such as the Charles Camsell in Edmonton and the Moose Factory Hospital serving eastern Hudson Bay. All residents of the Northwest Territories are covered by hospital insurance.

Good air transportation permits the speedy evacuation of patients needing specialized care to Montreal, Toronto, Winnipeg or Edmonton.

The Eastern Arctic Patrol has been stepped up, and now in place of a single doctor on a ship that was primarily a supply ship, a medical party comprising three or four medical officers, usually a specialist or two, such as an ophthamologist and a radiologist, an X-ray technician, two dentists, and nurses and helpers totalling a medical party of about 16 members, make this trip each year.

The patrol of recent years, by the department of transport vessel the *C. D. Howe* with its helicopter to bring aboard any persons unable to come on their own, is now primarily a medical mission, giving much more complete coverage of Hudson Strait, Baffin Island, and the neighbouring islands, as far as Grise Fjord and Resolute Bay, than was formerly carried out. Patients requiring treatment are taken on board and evacuated south by air from available bases.

A campaign to train native health workers has proved valuable and interesting. Various communities are asked to select a candidate, and a group, so selected, are brought to central points, usually where a hospital is located, for example Cambridge Bay. These persons are paid so that the family at home does not suffer if the recruit happens to be the bread-winner. A course of intensive instruction for about three months is given after which the trainees go back to their communities, and are put on salary to work under the direction of the departmental medical or nursing personnel. This program seems to be a successful one.

Even with all the difficulties inherent in the region and the shortages of personnel, a high percentage of the people have received

Salk vaccine for polio, vaccination against smallpox, and inoculation against diphtheria, whooping cough and tetanus, and an active program of B.C.G. vaccination has begun to raise resistance to tuberculosis infection. A campaign of measles vaccination has been organized. Saturation surveys are carried on throughout the north, the objective being to X-ray everyone, at least once a year, and to keep vaccinations and inoculations up-to-date.

These activities have produced tangible results. Early surveys showed an incidence of 12 per cent of the population having active disease requiring hospital treatment. This has now fallen to one per cent. Tuberculosis, once the leading cause of death, has moved to ninth place. Best indication of all of the success of health programs and preventive medicine is the fact that the death rate is decreasing steadily and natural increase is on the upswing. The population of the Territories is now rising at the rate of four per cent per year by natural increase alone, which means that it will double in 18 years. The crude overall birth rate is 49.2 per thousand, practically twice the average national rate. The crude death rate of 8.6 per thousand at last calculation was the lowest ever recorded in the Territories.

Yet, environmental factors, the age-old enemies, have not yet been conquered. The fact that injuries and violence remain the leading cause of death (24 per cent) in the Territories bespeaks the harshness of this land, as do the second and third ranking factors, disease of the respiratory system and diseases of infancy.

Elaborate plans have been prepared to further improve health facilities in the north, which range from improvement of basic treatment installations to medical research into the health problems characteristic of the area. Specifically they call for better communications for isolated communities; voice contact with medical consultants on a 24-hour a day basis; visual contact when technically feasible; the recruitment of more medical and auxiliary personnel, together with programs of further training and refresher courses; regular periodic visits to northern stations by medical specialists for consultations and seminars; training of indigenous residents of the Territories in the healing arts at progressively more advanced levels. Specialized courses for the training of health personnel in the specific knowledge and skills required for practice in the north have been suggested for the future medical school at

Memorial University, St. John's, Newfoundland and at teaching hospitals serving as base hospitals to field facilities in the north.

One way of defeating the traditional health hazards is to provide adequate housing to all residents. This problem is now being attacked by the department of northern affairs and other government agencies.

The first inhabitants of the Territories, with the meagre means at their disposal, but with courage and ingenuity, had evolved a way of life which insured their survival in this inhospitable land. Modern resources and technology now must bring this level above mere survival, to healthy, progressive communities. Only then will our northern regions and their people be truly part of Canada.

DR. PERCY MOORE, *Retired. Formerly Director of Indian and Northern Health Services, Department of National Health and Welfare. Born Kemptville, Ontario. M.D., University of Manitoba, 1931. Medical Supervisor Fisher River Indian Agency, 1931. Assistant Superintendent and Acting Superintendent Indian Medical Services, 1938-45. Past President, Canadian Tuberculosis Association.*

PROF. TOM BOAG

Mental Health in the North

> *Since time began the Eskimo and Indian*
> *people have had mental health*
> *problems. Thus arises the question: does the*
> *break-away from the traditional*
> *way of life increase their susceptibility to*
> *mental illness?*

Although the modern opening up of the north had begun during
World War II, in essence the arctic still remained a large area of
hostile climate, sparsely occupied by Eskimos, penetrated by ex-
peditionary groups from the south for relatively short periods, and
dotted with small, isolated outposts of white men — weather stations, Hudson's Bay posts, police posts, missions, and so on.

So, although the Eskimo has had a long history of contact with
whites until the last decade or so it was intermittent and not overwhelming; they maintained, relatively intact, their own culture
with its value systems and world perspectives which are so intimately related to patterns of mental health or illness. Until recently
they had borrowed aspects of our technology and values, incor-
porated them into their own system, but now they seem to be in
the process of being assimilated into our own southern Canadian
culture. With greater numbers of white people moving into the
north, and with better communications, the larger settlements and
towns are developing toward the patterns of southern Canada with
a concomitant decrease in the importance of the special, isolated
groups composed predominantly of single men.

It seems fair to predict that the north will rapidly lose those
features which made it a special and different environment with
special and different mental health problems and it will come to
resemble much more closely other parts of Canada albeit with its
own pattern of regional variation. However, this process will take
time, and for some time to come threads drawn from the past will

weave an important part of the newly developing pattern, so that it is of more than just historical interest to go back and take a look at mental health in the north as I first saw it 15 years ago and as it can be extracted from the literature of the past.

If we turn back to look at this, we can start by asking ourselves what is special to this geographical area that may lead to characteristically different patterns of mental health. Without attempting to be exhausive, I would suggest that we may list two sets of factors: first, the special stresses imposed by the geography of the region; and, second, the cultural characteristics of the human groups found there.

In the first set we can include the rigors of the climate — cold, snow and winter darkness, the restrictions imposed by the measures needed to adapt to the climate, the isolation, and the relative deprivation of many satisfactions we take for granted. In the second set we can include the traditional cultures of the native peoples, particularly the Eskimo, and the rather varied frontier groups of white men, partly self-selected, and partly officially selected for special purposes.

The environmental stresses necessarily have to be accommodated in the complexities of the Eskimo's way of life, but we can't assume that because we, from our experience, generally fear the cold and darkness of the arctic, the Eskimo will also react in the same way. It seems clear that the meanings of these climatic stresses are very different to him and don't have any simple relationship to emotional stress and strain, so I shall defer further discussion of them for the moment. We don't know very much about the patterns of mental illness in the Eskimo. On the basis of what we do know, and generalizing comparative studies of peoples around the world, we can expect to see the same general types of illness but there will be differences in the frequency with which they occur, and the symptom patterns of a given illness may be modified in conformity with the overall personality patterns of the culture. We have no idea of the frequency of mental illness in the past but, as treatment facilities have become available, we can at least count those who receive treatment. It seems that the frequency of mental illness is approximating that in Canada as a whole. It's hard to evaluate this since so many other changes are taking place in the Eskimo's way of life. He is subjected to the stress of culture change and it's a common finding in other parts of the world that, as simpler non-western societies adopt western culture, their rates of mental illness tend to rise to the same as ours and the symptomatic pictures come to resemble those common in our society.

It has been suggested, on the basis of small numbers of cases, that patterns of violence directed against the self or others are common in mentally ill Eskimos. Also, some studies of localized groups of Eskimos have demonstrated consistently very high rates of suicide and homicide; and that's about as far as the figures go. In addition to these kinds of variation, we recognize the occurrence of a special idiosyncratic illness in Eskimos not known to occur elsewhere in the world, the well-known "pibloktoq" or "arctic hysteria," in which the victim runs into the winter night tearing off his or her clothes, but we shouldn't yield to the temptation to explain this behaviour simply as a reaction to cold or dark. Another such special localized illness has occurred among the Cree and Ojibwa — the so-called "Witiko" or "Windigo" psychosis, which is associated with cannibalism. With the breakdown of traditional culture some Eskimo communities are showing major strains, but there are also examples of adaptation occurring successfully in the right circumstances, and it appears that in these cases successful social integration is reflected in good personal integration and mental health in the members of the community. In the most fragmented Eskimo communities, particularly those on the outskirts of white communities, we can see some evidence of the usual rising indices of social disintegration: drunkenness, promiscuity, and so on.

In dealing with the old pattern of white settlement, that is to say expeditions or isolated posts, the major concern has always been with the matter of selection of the best men for these assignments. It does seem that interpersonal problems in these groups are frequent, judging from personal accounts, though they rarely find their way into print. There is no convincing evidence that they are worse than in any such special and isolated groups living under stress in other parts of the world.

It may be that the isolation and difficulties in communication have made such upheavals particularly disrupting and particularly expensive to remedy, so that this accounts for the concern rather than an undue frequency. In spite of the efforts that have been made, I don't know of any particularly helpful guides to selection that go beyond the usual prescription of a stable adaptable individual who is well motivated, the usual general picture of a good man for a job anywhere. The only special consideration which may be of relevance is the motivation and or ability to undertake some form of active mastery of the arctic environment. It seems that this may protect against the withdrawal into shelter which precedes many difficulties. With regard to rates of mental illness among the white population, again we have few figures, but it seems that they approach those for Canada as a whole as the white population changes to become a more and more typical segment of Canadian society. However, the figures are still lower than for Canada generally, partly because there is still an unduly high proportion of selected young, healthy males and partly because there is still a high proportion of such people on relatively short-term assignments who, if they need help, may defer seeking this until they return to the south.

Finally, what of the future? As I stated earlier, the prediction for the white population must be that it will come to resemble that of the rest of Canada more and more clearly and that, as it does so, its mental health problems and its services will follow the same path. The fate of the Eskimo is an open question. They are in a difficult period of transition. Some groups show the evidence of social breakdown and concomitant behaviour problems. Other groups appear to be making good progress towards a stable adaptation to our society. The risk is that, to the extent that they are only partially integrated, they may become a deprived minority living on the fringes of white society with all the implications of this for poor mental health.

PROF. TOM BOAG, *Professor of Psychiatry and Chairman of the Department, University of Vermont College of Medicine. Born Liverpool, 1922. M.B., Ch.B., University of Liverpool, 1944. Training in Psychiatry, McGill, 1949-1954. Training in Psychoanalysis, McGill, 1954-1958. Field trips with Queen's University Arctic Expedition. Member, Canadian Psychiatric Association, Canadian Psychoanalytic Association. Fellow, Academy of Psychoanalysis, etc.*

ERNEST A. COTE

Conclusion

What is Canada's north like today? What are the essential factors which will shape and influence its future development?

About 40,000 people live in the Yukon and the Northwest Territories. They share 40 per cent of the land mass of Canada, that is to say, something in the order of a million and a half square miles. It should be said that the western part — the Yukon and parts of the Mackenzie Valley — is better served than the eastern and high arctic. There are trees in the western part which hold and nurture the soil, and this area seems to have suffered less from the ravages of the last ice age which scraped away so much of our northern soil, leaving only rock, sand, gravel, and of course, the minerals which lie beneath the soil. The arctic is characterized by barren lands, harsh climate and great distances with few communication systems.

In the west only one navigable river leads to the northern sea; this is the Mackenzie River. In the east, there is of course the sea route via Hudson Bay, but arctic transportation in Canada must rely heavily on modern technology, including air transport, an expensive proposition.

The northern territories are very rich in natural resources; there are extensive stands of timber, fisheries and possibly as much as six million kilowatts of hydro-electrical potential.

Although mapping and geological surveys have been pushed ahead vigorously the value of the Canadian northern storehouse has not yet been fully assessed. The oil and gas potential shows great promise. As an example, the total volume of oil and gas-bearing sedimentary rocks for the western Canadian provinces and the Northwest Territories and Yukon has been estimated at about 1.6 million cubic miles, of which one million cubic miles are thought to lie in the Yukon and Northwest Territories, and mainly in the Arctic Islands.

What does this mean to the oil picture? It's estimated that by 1985 Canada could produce more than one million barrels of crude oil per day for use by Canadian refineries and a further 700,000 barrels per day for export; this is almost double the present rate of production. Where new deposits are found in commercial quantities, it may take anywhere up to five years to go into production. Oil companies are busy all over Canada, including the high arctic, exploring potential deposits.

Mining is also being exposed to new and varied developments. Very large iron ore deposits have been located in both territories. The Snake River deposit on the Yukon-Northwest Territories border is one of the largest in the world and the Mary River deposit, in northern Baffin Island, is one of the richest ever discovered in Canada. The big new lead and zinc development at Pine Point is well established. A new asbestos mine is being opened up near Dawson city in the Yukon and tungsten mining has been renewed in the Northwest Territories where excellent reserves are known to exist.

Research is a vital factor in the plans for northern progress. Conditions are admittedly difficult. The problems are perhaps harder to solve in the Canadian north than those facing other countries, including the U.S.S.R.

This means that we must acquire more knowledge about the land and its people and find better ways of doing things. We have only to think of the implications of nuclear-powered cargo-carrying submarines, operating under the ice, for the transportation of oil or air-cushioned vehicles, which move over water, level land, and ice, and operate during break-up and freeze-up, to realize only a few of the new horizons that are coming into view.

If these resources are really to benefit the people of the north, they must participate in their exploitation. The keys to ensure this participation by the northerner are, of course, education, housing, health and well-being, and progress towards self-government.

Among the first objectives of government is the participation of the northerners in their own development. The government is striving to provide schooling . . . vocational and occupational training and university opportunities to enable the people of the north to be competitive in the 20th century.

Nearly 85 per cent of school age children of the Northwest Territories are now receiving schooling; this is five times the figure of ten years ago. The pace of the education program as well as the scope and quality of the curriculum will be accelerated in the years to come. Every effort is being made to ensure that education will be even more closely adapted to the needs of the northern people for the future in their own homeland.

The health services in the north are vital; they are staffed by dedicated people with high professional skills, geared to the requirements of the variety in climate and living conditions of this land. To insure success of education, and health and welfare programs, it is necessary to raise the living standards of the people; a fundamental requirement for this is adequate housing. A plan has been adopted to provide 1,500 new homes for the Eskimo and Indian population over the next five years. A staff, supplied with sufficient funds, will make a concentrated effort to eliminate, as quickly as possible, the appalling substandard housing which still characterizes many arctic communities.

But these social services must be based on the resources of the north. Over the next decade, a $10 million annual road building program will be developed. This program has provision for north-south transportation within the Territories and with the provinces. For the first time there will be a permanent east-west link between the Territories. It is hoped that all potential areas of resource development will be within 200 miles of the nearest permanent road.

The ideal situation would be complete self-support of the people who live in the north. This objective, however, can and I am sure will be achieved by dynamic and intelligent exploitation of the land-based resources. The co-operatives for marketing Eskimo art and handicrafts are but one small example; they will continue to play an important role in achieving the objective of local employment and self-sufficiency for the scattered population.

The construction advances of the last two or three years are part of a continuum. Canada's new dimension lies in the north. Canadians have so much to gain in embarking on bold plans to develop its resources.

As Canada faces her second century, her north — the Yukon and Northwest Territories — will provide not only a good living for the people of these Territories, but will give all of Canada greater depth, wealth and stature.

If all Canadians look upon the north as part of their Canadian inheritance, it can be a truly uniting factor transcending factions and fractioning tendencies into which our restive regional nationalisms so often push us. The north can be one of Canada's great sources of inspiration and unity.

Bibliography

ANDERSON, J. W., *Fur Trader's Story*, Ryerson, Toronto, 1961.

ANDREWS, C. L., *The Eskimo and his Reindeer in Alaska*, The Caxton Printers Ltd., Caldwell, Idaho, 1939.

ANDREWS, R. C., *Whalehunting with Gun and Camera*, Appleton, New York, c 1916.

ARBES, SAUL, "Social Change and the Eskimo Co-operative at George River, Quebec", Northern Co-ordination and Research Centre, Department of Indian Affairs and Northern Development, Ottawa.

ARMSTRONG, T., *The Northern Sea Route*, Cambridge University, 1952.

ARMSTRONG, T., *The Russians in the Arctic*, Methuen, London, 1958.

ARMSTRONG, T., *Russian Settlements in the North*, Cambridge University, 1965.

BAIRD, P. D., "Expeditions to the Canadian Arctic", *Beaver*, March, June, 1949.

BALIKCI, ASEN, "Development of Basic Socio-Economic Unities in Two Eskimo Communities", National Museum of Canada, *Bulletin 202*, 1964.

BALIKCI, ASEN, "Some Acculturative Trends Among Eastern Canadian Eskimos", *Anthropologica*, Vol. 2, No. 2, 1960.

BALIKCI, ASEN, "Suicidal Behaviour Among the Netsilik Eskimos", *North*, July-August, 1961.

BALIKCI, ASEN, "Relations inter-ethniques à la Grande Rivière de la Baleine, Baie d'Hudson, 1957", National Museum of Canada, *Bulletin 173*, 1961, pp. 64-107.

BALLANTYNE, R. M., *Ungava*, London, 1857.

BIRKETT-SMITH, KAJ, *The Eskimos*, revised by C. Daryll Forde, London, 1959.

BLACKMORE, MRS. ANAUTA, *Land of the Good Shadows*, John Day, New York, 1940.

BLADEN, V. W., "Canadian Population and Northern Colonization", Royal Society of Canada, Toronto, 1962.

BOAG, T. J., "The White Man in the Arctic: a Preliminary Study of Problems of Adjustment", *American Journal of Psychiatry*, December, 1952.

BOAG, T. J., and WITTKOWER, E. D., *Progress In Psychotherapy*, Vol. 3, 1958.

BOWLES, GORDON E., ed., "Peace River Chronicles", Historical Society News.

BROWN, M., GREEN, J. E., BOAG, T. J., and KUITUNEN-EKBAUM, "Parasitic Infections in the Eskimos in Igloolik, NWT", *Canadian Journal of Public Health*, December, 1950.

BROWN, W. E., "Tractors in the Arctic", *Polar Records*, No. 11, Cambridge University, January, 1936.

BUCK, KEITH W., and HENDERSON, J. F., "The Role of Mineral Resources in the Colonization of the North", Royal Society of Canada, 1962.

CANADIAN BROADCASTING CORPORATION, "CBC Northern Service", *North,* July-August, 1962.

CARD, BRIGHAM Y., *The Metis in Alberta Society,* University of Alberta, Edmonton, 1963.

CLAIRMONT, D. H., "Deviance among Indians and Eskimos in Aklavik NWT", *Report 63-9,* Northern Co-ordination and Research Centre, Department of Indian Affairs and Northern Development, 1963.

DALLYN, F. J., and FRAZER, G. EARLE, "A Study of Attitudes towards Indians and People of Indian Descent", Canadian Council of Christians and Jews Inc., Winnipeg, 1957.

DAMAS, DAVID, "Igluligmiut Kinship and Local Grouping: a Structural Approach", National Museum of Canada, *Bulletin 196,* 1963.

DAMAS, DAVID, "The Patterning of the Iglulingmiut Kinship System", *Ethnology,* October, 1964.

DE WEERDT, MARK M., "The Court of Appeal of the Northwest Territories", *North,* September-October, 1962.

DICKENS, H. B., and PLATTS, R. E., "Housing in Northern Canada: some recent development", *Polar Records,* September, 1960, pp. 223-230.

DUNBAR, MOIRA, and GREENAWAY, KEITH R., *Arctic Canada from the Air,* Queen's Printer, Ottawa, 1956.

DUNNING, R. W., "Ethnic Relations and the Marginal Man in Canada", *Human Organization,* Vol. 18, No. 3, 1959.

ELLIS, C. DOUGLAS, *Spoken Cree,* part 1, Department of Missions, Anglican Church of Canada, Toronto, 1962.

ELLIS, C. DOUGLAS, "Tagmemic Analysis of a Restricted Cree Text", *Journal of the Canadian Linguistic Association,* Vol. 6, No. 1, Spring 1960.

ELLIS, C. DOUGLAS, "A note on Okima•hka•n: the Role of the Chief as seen through Cree Eyes", *Anthropological Linguistics,* Vol. 2, No. 3, March 1960.

ELLIS, C. DOUGLAS, "The so-called Interrogative Order in Cree", *International Journal of American Linguistics,* Vol. 27, No. 1, April 1961.

FAIRLEY, T. C., "Oil Chasers of the Far North", *North,* November-December, 1961.

FORD, JAMES A., "Eskimo Prehistory in the Vicinity of Point Barrow, Alaska", the American Museum of Natural History, *Anthropological Papers,* 1959.

FRIED, J., "A Survey of the Aboriginal Populations of Quebec and Labrador", *Eastern Anthropological Series No. 1,* McGill University, Autumn 1955.

FREUCHEN, PETER, *Arctic Adventure,* Farrar and Rinehart, New York, c 1935.

FREUCHEN, PETER, *I Sailed with Rasmussen,* Messner, New York, c 1958.

FREUCHEN, PETER, *Vagrant Viking,* Messner, New York, 1953.

GARNER, SIR SAVILLE, "Northern Tour", *North,* May-June, 1961.

GIDDINGS, J. LOUIS, *The Archaeology of Cape Denbigh,* Brown University, Bicentennial publications, 1964.

GIRAUD, MARCEL, *"Le Métis Canadien: son rôle dans l'histoire des provinces de l'Ouest,* Institut d'Ethologie, Paris, 1945.

GRABURN, N. H. H., "Cross-Cousins Marriage and the Naskapi", Paper given at the annual meeting of the American Anthropological Association, Denver, 1955.

GRABURN, N. H. H., "Naskapi Kinship", in preparation for *Ethnology,* 1966.

GRABURN, N. H. H., "The Indians and Eskimos of Ungava", *Inter-Ethnic Monographs No. 1,* Wiley & Co., New York, 1967.

GREUNING, ERNEST H., *The State of Alaska,* Random House, New York, 1954.

HARP, ELMER JR., *The Cultural Affinities of the Newfoundland and Dorset Eskimos,* National Museum of Canada, 1964.

HARRINGTON, RICHARD, *The Face of the Arctic,* Schuman, New York, c 1952.

HEARNE, SAMUEL, *A Journey to the Northern Ocean,* edited by Richard Glover, MacMillan, Toronto, 1958.

HELM, JUNE, and LURIE, NANCY O., "The Subsistence Economy of the Dogrib Indians of Lac La Matre in the Mackenzie District of the Northwest Territories", Northern Co-ordination and Research Centre, Department of Indian Affairs and Northern Development, Canada, 1961.

HELM, JUNE, "The Lynx Point People: the Dynamics of a Northern Athapaskan Band", National Museum of Canada, *Bulletin 176,* 1961.

HELM, JUNE, and LURIE, NANCY O., "The Dogrib Hand Game", National Museum of Canada, *Bulletin 205,* 1966.

HILDES, J. A., "Medical Problems in the Arctic", *Manitoba Medical Review,* October 1959, pp. 581-583.

HILDES, J. A., "Health Problems in the Arctic", *Canadian Medical Association Journal,* December 10, 1960, pp. 1255-1257.

HOBART, C. W., "Under-achievement among Minority Group Students: an Analysis and Proposal", *Phylon,* second quarter, 1963.

HOBART, C. W., "Non-Whites in Canada: Indians, Eskimos, Negroes", in Laskin, *Social Problems, a Canadian Profile,* MacMillan, Toronto, 1964.

HOBART, C. W., and BRANT, CHARLES, "Socio-cultural Conditions and Consequences of Native Education in the Arctic: a Cross-National Comparison", submitted to *Canadian Review of Anthropology and Sociology.*

HONINGMANN, JOHN J., "Intercultural Relations at Great Whale River", *American Anthropologica,* Vol. 54, No. 4, 1952.

HONINGMANN, JOHN J., *Culture and Personality,* Harper Bros., New York, 1954.

HONINGMANN, JOHN J., "Social Networks in Great Whale River", National Museum of Canada, *Bulletin 178,* Ottawa, 1962.

HONINGMANN, JOHN J., *Understanding Culture,* Harper and Row, New York, 1963.

HONINGMANN, JOHN J., and HONINGMANN, IRMA, *Eskimo Townsmen,* Canadian Research Centre for Anthropology, University of Ottawa, 1966.

HOWARD, J. K., *Strange Empire: a Narrative of the Northwest,* Wm. Morrow, New York, 1952.

HULLEY, CLARENCE C., *Alaska 1741-1953,* Binfors and Mort, Portland, Oregon, 1953.

HYDE, MICHAEL, *Arctic Whaling Adventures,* Oxford University Press, London, 1955.

JENNESS, DIAMOND, "Eskimo Administration: 1, Alaska", Arctic Institute of North America, *Technical paper, No. 10,* Montreal, 1964.

JENNESS, DIAMOND, *Dawn in Arctic Alaska,* University of Minnesota Press, c 1957.

JENNESS, DIAMOND, *People of the Twilight,* MacMillan, Toronto, 1928.

JENNESS, DIAMOND, "The Indian Background of Canadian History", National Museum of Canada, *Bulletin 65,* 1955.

LOTZ, J. R., ed., "Government Research Surveys in the Canadian North, 1955-1962", Northern Co-ordination and Research Centre, Department of Indian Affairs and Northern Development, Ottawa, 1963.

MACDONALD, RONALD, ed., *Arctic Frontier,* University of Toronto, 1966.

MACKAY, DOUGLAS, *The Honourable Company,* McLellan and Stewart, Toronto, 1936; Revised by Mrs. Alice Mackay, 1949.

MACLEOD, MARGARET A., and MORTON, W. L., *Cutbert Grant of Grantown, Warden of the Plains of Red River,* McLellan and Stewart, Toronto, 1963.

MOLLOY, ARTHUR, "Arctic Science and the Nuclear Submarine", *Arctic,* June 1962, pp. 87-91.

NICHOLSON, CDR. J. H., "The Nuclear Submarine and the Arctic", *North,* November-December, 1962.

PATTERSON, R., *Far Pastures,* Gray's Publishing, Sidney, B.C., 1963.

RICH, E. E., *History of the Hudson Bay,* Hudson Bay Record Society, London, 1958-59.

ROBERTSON, R. GORDON, "The Future of the North", *North,* March-April, 1961, pp. 1-13.

SIVERTZ, B. G., "The North as a Region", *Resources for Tomorrow Conference,* Vol. 1, Section 4, Queen's Printer, Ottawa, 1961, pp. 561-577.

SIVERTZ, B. G., "Cultural Change: Fast or Slow", *North,* September-October, 1963.

SLOBODIN, RICHARD, "Band Organization of the Peel River Kutchin", National Museum of Canada, *Bulletin 179,* 1962.

SMITH, I. NORMAN, ed., *The Unbelievable Land,* Queen's Printer, 1964.

SPENCER, ROBERT F., "The North Alaska Eskimo: a Study in Ecology and Society", Bureau of America Ethnology, *Bulletin 171,* 1959.

STEFANSSON, VILHJALMUR, *Explorers Club Tales,* Tudor, New York, 1940.

STEFANSSON, VILHJALMUR, *The Fat of the Land,* MacMillan, New York, c 1956.

STEFANSSON, VILHJALMUR, *The Friendly Arctic,* MacMillan, New York, 1921.

VALENTINE, V. F., "The Métis of Northern Saskatchewan", Department of Natural Resources, Regina, 1955.

VAN DEN STEENHOVEN, GEERT, "Legal Concept among the Eskimos of Pelly Bay, Northwest Territories", *Report 59-3,* Northern Co-ordination and Research Centre, Department of Indian Affairs and Northern Development, Ottawa, 1959.

VANSTONE, JAMES W., *Point Hope, an Eskimo Village in Transition,* University of Washington Press, 1962.

VANSTONE, JAMES W., *Changing Culture in the Snowdrift Chipewyan,* National Museum of Canada, 1965.

VALLEE, FRANK, "Kabloona and Eskimo in the Central Keewatin", Northern Co-ordination and Research Centre, Department of Indian Affairs and Northern Development, Ottawa, 1962.

VALLEE, FRANK, "Notes on the Co-operative Movement and Community Organization in the Canadian Arctic", *Arctic Anthropology,* Vol. 2, 1964.

WILLIAMSON, GEOFFREY, *Changing Greenland,* London, 1953.

WILSON, J. TUZO, *IGY: The Year of the New Moon,* Longmans, Toronto, 1961.

WATSON, J. B., "Caste as a Form of Acculturation", *Southwestern Journal of Anthropology,* Vol. 19, No. 4, 1963, pp. 356-379.

BEAVER, Published by the Hudson's Bay Company, Winnipeg 1, Manitoba. This magazine features popular and historical articles on the Canadian west and the north.

CANADIAN GEOGRAPHICAL JOURNAL, This magazine, published by the Royal Canadian Geographical Society, 54 Park Avenue, Ottawa 4, frequently features articles on the Canadian Arctic.

NORTH, Published by the Queen's Printer for the Northern Administration Branch, Department of Indian Affairs and Northern Development. This magazine contains popular articles on the North.

POLAR RECORDS, Published by the Scott Polar Research Institute, Cambridge, England. This contains technical and scientific articles and papers, short summaries of the work of polar expeditions and a bibliography. Published three times a year.

Index

Adult education, 46
Agriculture, *see* Farming
Aklavik, 39, 40, 41, 45, 50, 52, 124, 132
Alaska, 2, 3, 10, 32-3, 39, 50, 85-9
Alberta, 95, 111
Albany, *see* Fort Albany
Alert, 69
Algonkian language group, 101
Amderma, 67
Amundsen Gulf, 60
Anchorage, 52, 85, 86, 87
Archangel, 65, 67
Arctic, The, *passim*
Arctic Bay, 52
Arctic char, 68
Arctic fox, *see* White fox
Arctic hysteria, 139
Arctic Islands, 95, 141
Arctic Ocean, 54
Asbestos, 142
Ashiarmuit, 55
Athapaskan language group, 101
Atlin, 49
Aviation, 57

Baffin Bay, 61
Baffin Island, 2, 11, 35, 73, 97, 134, 142
Baker Lake, 52
Baleen, 31, 32
Ballantyne, R. M. *Ungava,* 123
Barents Sea, 64, 65
Barren Lands, 21
Barrow Strait, 60
Barter Island, 60
Bathurst Inlet, 117
Bearded seal, 2
Beaufort Sea, 29, 32, 60
Beaver Indians, 101
Beaver, 26
Bell Telephone Company, 51, 52
Belousov, 66
Beluga whales, *see* White whales
Bering Sea, 29
Bering Strait, 2, 29, 31, 32, 60, 64, 66
Berry, Matt 57
Birth rate, 135
Blackfoot Indians, 110
Blue geese, 9
Bonanza Creek, 49
Borisa Vil Strait, 66
Bowhead whales, 29, 30-1, 32-3
British Columbia, 85
Brown, Roy, 57
Bubbler system, 62, 70

C.N.T., 51
C. D. Howe, 62, 134
Cambridge Bay, 51, 52, 60, 118, 134
Canada, *passim*
Canada geese, 9
Canadian-American Joint Arctic
    Weather Stations, 50, 52, 61
Canadian Broadcasting Corporation.
    Northern Service, 50
Canadian Coast Guard, 61, 62
Canadian National Telecommunica-
    tions, 51
Canol Project, 50
Cape Dorset, 45
Cape Zhelaniya, 64
Caribou, xv, xvii, 2, 11, 69, 70, 102
Caribou Eskimos, 4, 92, 94
Carrier Indians, 102
Cassiar, 55
Central Eskimos, 115-17
Charles Camsell Hospital, 134
Chesterfield Inlet, 50, 52, 57, 61, 132,
    133
Chipewyan Indians, 101, 110
Chukchee, *see* Chukchi
Chukchi (tribe), 82
Chukchi Peninsula, 30, 32
Chukchi Sea, 64
Churchill, 2, 50, 61, 120, 121, 132
Churchill River, 8, 112
Co-operative Union of Canada, 47
Co-operatives, 24, 43, 45-8, 143
Copper Eskimos, 117
Coppermine, 50, 117
Coronation Gulf, 3, 60
Cossacks, 81
Cree Indians, 12, 15, 16, 17, 101, 110,
    139
Cree language, 18
Cultural relativity, 72-5
Culture shock, xvi

DEW Line, 50, 57, 120
Dawson, 34, 41, 50, 52, 142
Dease Strait, 60
Death rate, 135
Déné Indians, 107-9
Denmark, 77
Department of National Health and
    Welfare. Northern Health Service,
    133, 134
Department of Northern Affairs and
    National Resources (Department of
    Indian Affairs and Northern Devel-
    opment), 47

Photo Credits

National Film Board — 1, 2, 3, 4, 5, 7, 8, 9, 10, 11, 13, 14, 15, 16, 17, 18, 19, 21, 26, 27, 28, 31, 33, 36, 37, 38, 39, 41, 42, 43, 44, 45, 46, 46A, 47, 49, 50, 51, 52, 53, 55, 56, 57, 59, 60.

E. Bork — 6, 23, 48.

Hudson's Bay Company — 20, 37A, 40.

A. C. Au

Public Arch

D. David Sla

Polar Equidistant Projection
Reproduced From
Northern Hemisphere Map
Produced by
Department of Mines and Technical Surveys,
1965